KEYS
HELPING
CHILDREN
DEAL WITH
DEATH AND
GRIEF

Joy Johnson

BARRON'S

Cover photo by Picture Perfect

Joy Johnson is cofounder, along with her husband, Dr. Marvin Johnson, of Centering Corporation, the nation's oldest bereavement resource center.

DEDICATION

To the KEY people in my life: Marv, the fantastic Six and their partners, the beautiful grandchildren, and the greats as well.

CREDIT

Material from *Life and Loss* by Linda Goldman is used with the author's permission.

© Copyright 1999 by Barron's Educational Series, Inc.

All inquiries should be addressed to:
Barron's Educational Series, Inc.
250 Wireless Boulevard
Hauppauge, New York 11788
http://www.barronseduc.com

Library of Congress Catalog Card No.: 99-25153
International Standard Book No. 0-7641-0963-4

Library of Congress Cataloging-in-Publication Data

Johnson, Joy.
   Keys to helping children deal with death and grief / Joy Johnson.
       p.   cm. — (Barron's parenting keys)
   Includes bibliographical references (p.   ) and index.
   ISBN 0-7641-0963-4
   1. Bereavement in children.   2. Grief in children.   3. Death—
Psychological aspects.   I. Title.   II. Series.
BF723.G75J64   1999
155.9'37—dc21   99-25153
                                           CIP

PRINTED IN THE UNITED STATES OF AMERICA
9 8 7 6 5 4 3 2 1

CONTENTS

INTRODUCTION

The most touching picture I have ever seen was taken around 1887. A young mother is holding a beautiful six- or seven-year-old girl in her arms. Both are dressed in their funeral finery. The little girl is dead, her long blonde ringlet curls falling over her mother's arm. The mother is looking directly into the camera and you cannot bear to look at her heartbroken eyes and you cannot bear to look away. This picture, more than anything I have seen, says grief is not an intellectual exercise. Grief breaks our hearts and hits us like ocean waves. It devastates us, diminishes us, changes us, and forces us to grow and become new people.

If you are reading this book, it's not likely you picked it up randomly at a major bookstore. You have a need for it. Whether you are a teacher, researcher, parent, or loved family member or friend, you want to know more about how to help, support, and guide children through grief. Reading about grief can be valuable. Hearing the children's stories and how their families responded reaches us at the heart level.

Throughout these pages, I'd like to share what I've learned over 25 years of working with grieving children and families, writing books for them and, with my husband, Dr. Marv Johnson, presenting workshops for caregivers and families called *Children Grieve, Too*.

If you are reading this because someone you love is dying or has just died, then read Parts Two, Five, and Ten first. Then sit with me. Have a good cup of coffee or flavored herb tea and learn about children and grief through the stories they have told us, the experiences they have lived, and the rich lessons they can teach.

Part One

TEACHING OUR CHILDREN

1

WHERE WE'VE BEEN

I'm from Iowa. In Iowa we joke that it's a state law that every family has to have a maiden aunt. We say that if you don't have a maiden aunt, the state sends you one. Our family's maiden aunt was Aunt Bess, a gutsy, sharp, independent woman who had a big pocket on her lap robe in the nursing home because she read trashy novels and hid them there.

Aunt Bess tells about being taken to her grandmother's home when she was four years old. The women in the kitchen were talking softly and weeping. Aunt Bess's mother took her to the main hall where the huge parlor doors stood tightly closed. Mamma sat her on a chair, told her to stay put, and went through the massive doors. She came out minutes later, crying. She hurried past her little daughter into the kitchen, never glancing at her child.

I'm sure Aunt Bess's little high-topped shoes clicked as she scampered across the floor to push open those big doors. She could barely get them open enough to squeeze inside to see what had made Mamma cry and rush away from her. Minutes later Aunt Bess showed up in the kitchen, pulling on her mother's apron. "You don't have to be scared, Mamma," she said. "It's just Grandpa in there being dead."

She had been protected from death and grief by a loving mother who didn't know how to tell a four year old what had happened to Grandpa. But Aunt Bess didn't need protection. She wasn't afraid. She just needed to be taught what death was and about the feelings that came when Mamma cried.

Even in times when death came frequently; when wagon trains buried body after body along the trail and pioneers and city folk alike died from disease every day, we protected our children. We protected them during the Great Depression when trains ran over the legs of vagrants riding the rails. We protected them during World War II when gold stars marked the homes of the dead. And we protected them in the 50s and the 60s right up until the 70s when we began to learn more about grief. Even now, who among us would not protect another, particularly a child, from hurt?

2

WHERE WE ARE NOW

It began in the early 1970s. Elisabeth Kubler-Ross did the research and wrote *On Death and Dying*. We learned that people who are dying experience shock, denial, anger, depression, and finally, acceptance. As we go from diagnosis to death, we experience loss. We who are dying lose everyone and everything, including ourselves. Along the same line, those of us who experience the death of a loved one go through the same dynamic of loss: shock, denial, anger, depression, and acceptance. After some time, we began to look at how children grieve. The parlor doors began to open.

Today children have tremendous choices and opportunities for support. There are:

- support groups for all ages
- hundreds of books and videos
- emotion dolls with whom to share feelings
- grief games and activities
- school counselors
- bereavement counselors
- resources and classes to help parents, teachers, and others
- full-time centers for grieving children.

Now we know children grieve, whether we try to "protect" them or not. We know we can't hide the truth about dying, grief, and death from them. We know that protecting them may mean they stuff their feelings and develop stomach aches, colds, and other problems. We can say now that it's normal for grades to drop some if a brother or sister or mom or dad or beloved grandparent dies. We know that children grieve, then play, grieve, then play . . . a lesson we could take to heart ourselves. We know about red flags and behavior that calls out for help. We know so much more than we used to know.

It's wonderfully refreshing to walk into a center for grieving children and enter their Emotion Commotion Room, where the walls are thickly padded, a punching bag hangs ready and willing to help fend off anger, and there are soft, spongy balls and shapes to throw against the wall. There's a cushion for just sitting and crying and there's a trained grief facilitator there, too, ready with a hug.

It's great to see a parent grab a book that tells her what is normal in children when they grieve and read in it that her family isn't mentally ill; because now we know that grief is not a mental illness or a pathological disease. We know that wetting the bed when you're eight years old and your favorite aunt dies isn't shameful, it may well be expected.

Most important of all, we know the best way to protect a child is not to pretend a death didn't happen, that grief isn't real. The best way to protect a child is to give them the keys to coping with grief, to walk through it with them, answering questions honestly and allowing them to be a part of this vital family event.

3

WHERE WE HOPE TO GO

We've made such great progress in learning and teaching about death and grief that there will come a day when the dark shroud of mystery will be removed from the image of death and we will talk freely about our fears and feelings.

A young minister was told, "You'd better be prepared for two things that will dominate your congregation and no one will talk about either: sex and death." We have found that once we begin to talk about death, others begin to share their experiences. They are rich, enlightening life events filled with learning and hope. We don't want to miss them.

When a funeral director held the funeral of a 100-year-old lady, he learned she had come to their small town as a teenager in a covered wagon. Her mother had left her china sitting beside the road when a heat wave endangered the oxen pulling the heavy load. First she buried her dog along the way and then was part of the circle of pioneers who buried a young wife who died in childbirth. The funeral director had known her for years and had never listened to her story. As we listen to stories of death and grief we hear true stories of life. We are moving to a time in which we listen, we write our stories, we share more of ourselves.

We cannot document prevention, but this new generation growing up will know better ways of integrating grief than did their parents. Children who have been given the keys of knowledge and guided through grief won't experience the illnesses and mental breakdowns our parents sometimes suffered because they were expected to act as if nothing happened after a cherished mate or beloved child died.

The future will find that people interviewed in shopping malls who are asked, "How long does it take to get over the death of a loved one?" won't answer, "Three weeks," as some did recently. Instead, the majority will know the answer is "never." We won't be afraid to remember and commemorate our family members who have died. We'll be more creative in the rituals that help us keep our bonds with those who live only in our hearts and memories.

Families will know about the keys they can give their children to make their lives not only strong but also full and rich and real. Death and grief are a part of our very being. To recognize that is, in a sense, to truly live.

Part Two

THE BASICS

4

START EARLY

There are times when we all need a short course. If someone you love is dying or has just died and there are children waiting for answers, read this short section for the basic training in teaching about death. If you're reading this book for general information, read it anyway. It's a good start, and the key to educating children about death and grief is to start early. Let it be natural.

Our granddaughter, Paris, was stung by a bee when she was two. After that, she pointed at and named every insect, "Beeee! Beeee!" Then one day she and I came across a dead bee lying on the sidewalk. "Beeee!" Paris said, pointing.

"Dead bee," I said. "Dead. Dead. See, the bee doesn't move now." I picked it up. It lay on its back, little legs in the air. Paris stared. "The bee can't feel now. Dead," I said again.

Paris put one tiny finger on the small wing. "Dead," she whispered. Even at age two she had somehow picked up my seriousness about the state of this one-time stinger. Her one whispered word said she knew deep down that this was important. Something very unique had happened to that bee.

Children do not naturally fear death. We instill it in them, put a black shroud around it and worry it into power. But when we really look at death and what it means, it takes on a dramatically different appearance. One of our friends, David Prowse, played Darth Vader in the *Star Wars* trilogy. There is no more frightening symbol of death and destruction than the powerful Lord of the Dark Side. Yet, if you get to know David, he'll tell you that as soon as his helmet was put over his head, his breath fogged up the goggles. The costume was extremely heavy. When he began to walk, his pants fell down. Throughout the films he wore white suspenders to keep Darth Vader's shorts from showing. Once we become acquainted with death, we realize it can't see all that well and its pants may fall down, too.

5

KNOW THE KEYS

As children grow and mature, they ask more detailed questions and need more complete answers. The best time to do any death education is when the event arises, whether it's the bee on the sidewalk, the bird in the street, or a dead pet. The teachable moment serves us well and doesn't need to be when a funeral occurs. If, however, a funeral is the first chance you have, you can recall times when the bird, pet, or dead bee entered the scene and go from there. The true keys to educating about death and grief are:

Be Honest

Children are people readers. They can tell if you're not telling them the truth. To say that Grandpa has gone on a long trip and will never be back is an out-and-out lie. The family member or well-meaning friend who tries to keep the truth from children is usually not the one who has to explain later why they were not respected enough or trusted enough to be told what really happened. Believe me—they will ask questions later.

A grandmother told how after her daughter completed suicide, she refused to tell her six-year-old grandson how his mother died. We asked a very important question, "Would you rather he hear it from you, knowing you love him and will be there to answer questions, or do you want him to hear it from a classmate during a moment of childhood cruelty or to overhear it during a family get-together?" When the child discovers the truth in this way, he's likely to feel betrayed, left out, that he's not-to-be-trusted, and deeply hurt.

"But how can I talk about such a terrible thing to a little boy?" the grandmother asked. She ended up going home, taking him on her lap, and saying, "Tony, there's something I want you to know and I want you to hear it from me because I love you and I'm here to answer your questions. Your mommy's mind was very, very sick. She wanted to die and couldn't think clearly. She killed herself and thought that would solve her problems. She didn't know it wouldn't solve anything, and she didn't know how sad it would make all of us." Grandma began to cry. Tony began to cry. They held each other. Now Tony can ask the questions he needs to ask, and Grandma doesn't have to waste the enormous amount of energy it takes to keep the skeleton in the closet.

Use Real Words

One of the resources listed in the back of this book is *Finding Grandpa Everywhere*. In it a little boy is rushed by his mother to his grandma's house because Grandma has lost Grandpa. He wonders how Grandma could lose someone as large as Grandpa. He assumes that all the people at Grandma's house are eating a lot because they need energy for the search. He thinks they're a little too dressed up to hunt through the woods, but he's prepared. He goes into a bedroom and puts on his child-sized army suit because he's a serious hunter. He'll find Grandpa! Of course, by the end of the book he understands that adults sometimes say *lost* to express the *loss* of a person through death, but that doesn't come easy to a young child.

Using words such as *lost*, *passed away*, or *passed on* can be deceptive to a child. Flowers die and people die. Saying "She's just asleep" can bring on nightmares and nightlights to many a child as well as virtually guaranteeing resistance at nap time.

Be Careful of God Talk

While it's very important to share your faith, be aware of how some things sound to a child. The four year old who suddenly starts acting out and being as mean and naughty as possible may well have heard that God wanted his brother because he was so good or that God needed another angel. The "God's will" talk can make God appear as a child or parent snatcher.

Before Chris's son Timmy died, she prepared Randy, his five-year-old brother. "Timmy will die," she said, "and then God will come and take his soul." She shared her belief, involved God in a healthy way and was honest. The family lived in North Dakota, on the windy, snow-driven northern plains. Every car in the hospital parking lot was a four-wheel-drive vehicle. Timmy died a peaceful, quiet death at 5 A.M. in his mother's arms. At 6 A.M., Randy came into the room. "Randy, Timmy died last night," Chris said, picking him up and hugging him. "Why didn't you wake me up?" Randy asked. "I didn't know just when he would die," his mom explained. "I wanted to see God!" Randy said, "Just what was God drivin' anyhow?" All this just goes to show that no matter how thorough you are, there will be questions you don't anticipate.

Share Your Feelings

Just as we feel a need to protect children, our children are protective of us. We have learned that by age two children know about grief and are taught how to act around adults who are grieving. Heather was not quite two when her baby sister died. Her mother told a friend how Heather never mentioned Jess, never talked about her. The friend looked puzzled. "She talks about her all the time when she's with us," she said. It was then that Heather's parents realized that each time Heather had mentioned her sister, they had cried. Heather didn't want them to be sad, so she stopped talking. Ray, Heather's father, took his little girl into her sister's bedroom and sat with her in the rocking chair. "Heather, it's okay to talk about Jess. We like to talk about Jess, and it's okay if we all cry, too. Your talking about her doesn't make us cry. You don't have to be afraid of our tears. Our tears are helping us feel better." And with that, Heather released. "Jessica! Jessica! Jessica!" she said, running out to the living room. There she asked her dad to pick her up so they could look at the pictures of Jessica on the wall. She got out the family album and for the first time in months the family shared their grief and their joy together.

Let Children Know That Feelings Are Okay

Feelings aren't good or bad; feelings are just feelings. It's what we do with them that counts and helps us move through grief.

Make Sure Children Know They Aren't Responsible for Our Tears

No one can "make" us cry. Emotions come from inside us. It's important to let children know that people will feel better after crying; that when we grieve it's not our job to take care of other people. It's our job to grieve.

Demonstrate Constructive Ways to Deal with Emotions

Anger can be frightening, and it's as natural in grief as the other feelings of sadness, guilt, and anxiety. Showing a child how to hit a bed with a tea-towel or even buying an old set of dishes and breaking them into a trash can releases anger. Children need to know there are constructive ways of letting off steam, whether it's playing a game of basketball or running around the block.

Provide Memories and Keepsakes

One of my greatest teachers was John Chesnutt. A counselor friend called and said, "I'm sending a dad to you. His wife is dying and he has a two year old and a five year old." In just a few minutes John walked through our door. He was young and handsome, a together kind of guy. And his wife was dying.

I made a stack of books for children and one for him. I started a stack on what to do when a loved one is dying, and he very gently pushed that stack aside. I caught on. "How long do you think your wife will live?" I asked. This was Friday and John answered, "Oh . . . she'll die this weekend."

I joke now that I felt as if I pinned him to the wall and yelled, "You have a lot to do!" We talked about involving the children in her funeral and about saying goodbye, and equally importantly, we talked about a "Mommy Box." John saved all of Bea's T-shirts, her jewelry, a hat she loved, treasures that were precious to her and put them in a special box. Both children knew they could go to the Mommy Box anytime and remember Mommy. John took Bea's watch and wedding ring off her wrist and finger when they went to say goodbye, threaded the narrow watch band through the lovely ring and put them in the box as well.

That was five years ago and Dara and Jefferson still visit the Mommy Box. They talk about Mommy and John keeps Bea's memory alive with stories and pictures. John's story is a rich one, and you'll meet him and his children more than once before you've finished reading this book.

Children will grieve when someone they love dies. They may need to have certain times when they are alone with their tears, certain times when they are held and cuddled. Most of all, they need to be reassured that the hurt will become less and finally turn into soft memories. They need to know there will be someone to care for them and listen to them no matter what, and they need to know that everyone they love isn't going to die. No matter whether your child is two or fifty-two, the best thing a parent can give during grief is a listen and a hug.

One of the most delightful books we've ever found is called *Lifetimes*, by Bryan Mellonie and Robert Ingpen. It's written for preschoolers and explains that in the beginning we are born. In the end we die. In between is called "living." Every living thing, no matter what or who it is, experiences this cycle of being born, living, and dying. So much happens during the living part. There can be sickness and accidents and usually things and animals and people become well again. But sometimes that isn't so. Sometimes even very young things and animals and people die, and that is part of a lifetime, too. It is a great little book because it shows us that death is natural and a part of life. Death is a sacred part of that which we call living and children need and deserve to learn and take part in the sacred.

Part Three

CONCEPTS
ACCORDING TO AGE

6

MAGICAL THINKING

We call it Magical Thinking because it reflects the feeling of power we either hope we have, wish we had, or are afraid we have. And it follows us from childhood right into adulthood. Some of it is delightful, some scary, some sad. When our daughter Jenny was in college, she used to have a little sign in her bedroom that said *Someday I will meet a handsome prince who will carry me away and marry me and make me happy ever after. Dream on!* That's delightful magical thinking.

Sad, guilt-ridden magical thinking popped out when I was having coffee with a beautiful young widow. Her heart-surgeon husband had been killed in an auto accident. Suddenly she said, "It's my fault." Then she caught herself. "Not really, I guess," she said, "It's just that every day when I kissed him goodbye, I told him to buckle up. That morning I was hurrying to get our daughter ready for her dance lesson and we just called goodbye to each other. I didn't tell him to buckle up."

Guilt is a part of magical thinking and guilt is also a part of grief. Magical thinking in children comes when they believe something they did or thought caused the death.

Allie Sims is a young writer and lecturer whose baby brother, Austin, died when she was just five. Her mother, Darcie, tells how they were working together in the kitchen one day when Allie was ten. Suddenly the little girl said, "I have a terrible secret and if I tell, no one will ever like me again. But I have to tell somebody because I just can't keep this inside any longer!" She started to cry. Darcie looked at her daughter and decided this was not a keep-on-peeling-the-carrots kind of conversation. The two women, one thirty and one ten, sat down in the middle of the kitchen floor. Allie looked at her mother through wet, weary eyes and said, "I killed my baby brother." Darcie's first reply was, "You couldn't have! I did!"

Allie had gone into Austin's room a few weeks after he was born, looked at him, and decided she didn't want a baby brother after all. "You can just go back where you came from!" she told him. When he died of a brain tumor, she was sure her words had made him die. Darcie, deep inside, had always felt that if she had just known more, gone to the doctor sooner, done something, Austin, lovingly called *Big A*, would have lived.

Whenever there is a death, children even as young as two, need to be told clearly and lovingly that they did not do or think anything that caused their loved one to die. They need to know it was not because they misbehaved, wished someone away, or had "bad" thoughts. There are times when this can be difficult. One father, who was good and caring and fun, often told his children, "You two are going to give me a heart attack!" Of course, he died when the oldest was twelve . . . of a heart attack.

Linda Goldman, who has worked with grieving children and spent much time and energy training adult parents and caregivers, tells about a three year old who quietly told her, "I killed my mommy." "How did you do that?" Linda asked. "The night before she died, she picked me up, so I killed her." Linda says that once the little girl could say that, they could talk about it. Once children can express their guilt, their magical thinking, we can work to correct it. Linda sat with her young friend and read *I Know I Made It Happen*, the little book by Marilyn Gryte, and helped lift a tremendous weight from tiny shoulders.

Guilt is almost always nonproductive. If children feel guilty about something they said or did before Grandma died, they can write a letter to her and apologize. They can be told clearly that Grandma understood. That is taking care of honest guilt. If their magical thinking tells them they caused the death, they need to be reassured that such a thing is not possible. If in fact, a child did cause a death, that is the time for professional counseling and help. That is the time to find someone who deals in bereavement as well as psychological support. (See Actual Responsibility in Key 20.)

Within each age, there is the concept of magical thinking. Keep it magically in mind as we talk about how children of different ages view death and experience grief.

7

CHILDREN'S CONCEPTS OF DEATH AND GRIEF

When I was five I fell in love with the song "When You Wish Upon A Star." I knew it could work for me. I solemnly stood on our front porch, found just the right star, and with faith way past the 100 percent mark, wished for a three-wheeled super-sized tricycle. At dawn the next morning I shot out of my bed, sped through my front door, and skidded to a stop on an empty porch. No trike. So much for stars. I had a very concrete concept at that age. As I grew, my concepts grew as well. At each age our ideas and our beliefs—in other words, our concepts—change.

Infants

Although babies obviously don't have language skills and can't think about or realize what is happening, they do respond to the grief of those around them. With any loss, especially that of a parent, the baby responds to the change in schedule, tension in those loving her, and the disruption in the household. We seem to have a built-in sense of sorrow in others, and this seems to be in both human and animals. As one of our friends said, "My little dog jumped on my lap and licked more than a million tears from my face." Maybe we human animals have the same instinct from birth on to respond to others.

What you can do:

- Keep to the baby's schedule as much as possible.
- Keep the baby in his own home and with as few people as possible caring for him.
- Do some extra cuddling.
- Talk to the infant as you hold her. Although she may not understand, it may help you a lot.

Keisha was three months old when her grandmother died. Her mother was extremely sad. Keisha began waking every two hours, cried at least twice as much as usual, and Mom began wearing a cloth diaper on her shoulder because the baby spit up so much. Finally, Keisha's mommy sat and rocked her, told her all about her grandmother, sang sad songs and cried, snuggling her head into Keisha's blanket. Gradually, things became normal again. Keisha's mother said, "She sensed I was sad. Someday I will tell her that even as a baby, we loved each other through grief, just as we love each other in happy times."

Toddlers—Ages Two to Five

Here is the delightful age of first language, first adventures, and very little idea of permanence. The two to five year old asks, "When is Daddy coming back?" They tend to become babies again when the family is grieving. They return to time when life was safer. Bedwetting, clinging, whining, and even having more illnesses are common. At this age, the child will grieve, play, grieve, play. Understanding is beginning to develop and children need to know they are an important part of the family. Magical thinking is very common now.

Remember, children this age do not have a sense of permanence. They may want to draw a picture and send it to Grandma in heaven. It's perfectly logical and all right to them to have you mail it. More than one envelope has held such a treasure and gone to the same address.

Don't be alarmed, either, if your two to five year old asks when you're going to pick up the sibling who died, or when you'll be going to visit Grandpa. This age thinks those who die will come back. Those concepts will change as the child matures.

What you can do:

• Be honest. Tell the child why the person died.
• Use words such as *dead* and *died.*
• Answer questions, knowing the questions may not come right away and may be asked over and over again as the child processes the answer.
• Explain what death is and what feelings the child may experience.
• Make sure they know it's okay to cry and okay to play as well.
• Be sure she knows she did not cause the death.
• Involve him as much as possible in funeral planning.
• Let her know someone will be there for her during the funeral and in the days ahead and after to give comfort and support.

Lana was four when her mother died. She became very clingy. She didn't want to go to preschool or be without her grandmother. She was experiencing what all of us experience when someone upon whom we depend dies: separation anxiety. She looked for her mother everywhere and cried whenever her grandmother had to leave her.

In addition to answering questions and taking Lana to the cemetery with her, Grandma began leaving something special with the little girl whenever she had to leave her with someone else . . . a set of keys, a purse filled with the usual things, a cherished sweater. Lana knew then that Grandma would come back and when she did, extra hugs would come, too.

Six to Nine

Children six to nine years old may know death is final but they may not want to admit it. The six to nine year old has watched cartoons. Even though Wile E. Coyote gets up every time the train runs over him, they've seen enough real and pretend violence on television and sometimes in their own lives to get an idea of permanence. They know what it's like to be afraid. They may overestimate their own magical thinking about causing the death and may think death is contagious. *If I play with Tanya now that her mother's died, my mother may die, too.* They don't know what to say or what to do when someone is grieving. In some ways, we adults become a lot like six to nine year olds.

This is an age when children can think death is a person, from the Grim Reaper figure to a really scary ghost. They can become preoccupied with their new knowledge about death and we're likely to hear the old tunes of *the worms crawl in, the worms crawl out.* The burial of dead birds can become elaborate and sensitive. The death of a loved pet can be sad and fascinating at the same time.

Our great old cat, Percy Greypaws, died when our children were eight, ten, and sixteen. He was a classy cat, even in his dying. He walked into the bathroom, lay down, and died. He died in the home of bereavement experts. We knew what to do. We covered him with a towel and waited for the kids to come home from school. When they did, we told them Percy had died and we gathered in the bathroom. Jim (16) held his body and said, "He was a great cat. Bye, Percy." He stroked the smooth gray fur. Jenny (10), whose cat he was, hugged him and cried into his chest. Janet (8) looked up and with an eager innocence asked, "When are we going to bury him?"

Words become important now because so many have double meanings. Dan Schaefer, funeral director and author, tells of a little boy who heard the word "soul" repeated over and over when his grandfather died. He later thought his grandfather was speaking to him from a shoebox in his closet. Instead of "soul" he had translated it into "sole."

What you can do:

- Ask what the child understands already.
- Work from his questions.
- Be honest and use words such as *dead* and *died*.
- Explain what feelings may come and that other children feel the same.
- Be sure she knows she didn't cause the death.
- Talk about any fears he has.
- Involve the child as much as possible in funeral planning, letting him know what will happen and when.
- Understand the need to play games that feature funerals, including the burial of dolls and other objects.

José seemed to grow up after his father died. His mother told him he was not the man in the family; it was his job to be a little kid, but he continued to seem more mature. He did start sleeping with a night light on, he drew pictures of cemeteries and caskets, and once in a while he was very embarrassed when he wet the bed. His mother put his dad's things in a Daddy Box and gave it to José and his sister. José took a bottle of aftershave from that box and kept it in his room. Every morning he would smell it. He said it helped him to remember his daddy.

We all need more attention and human contact when someone dies. The age six to nine marks the beginning of the end for sitting on laps, being cuddled and hugged, and crawling into bed with a parent when things get scary. Cuddle. Hug. Tell him you love him and you'll still be a family, no matter what.

Ten to Twelve

The *Tweens* they're sometimes called. Children this age are in that fragile area between small child and adolescent youth. Friends are terribly important to ten to twelve year olds and they often believe that grieving will make them seem *different*.

They want to be independent but know they can't yet make it on their own. They may fear abandonment, the death of others, and their own deaths. They worry about relationships: *Who will take care of Grandma now? How do we get the money we need?* They may seem withdrawn and distant, then suddenly become very close and vulnerable.

Here we have the interesting development of moral sense, of right and wrong. Death may be seen as a punishment. They may believe that because they weren't "good," Grandma died. One mother who sensed her son was troubled said very simply, "You know, a lot of kids think something they did or thought caused the death. What do you think of that idea?" From that question she learned her son was afraid of missing a movie with his friend and wished his grandmother would hurry up and die so he could be sure to go. He was dealing with death, guilt, and another common feeling: relief.

Children this age are becoming aware of cost and of being practical. They may seem very emotionally mature and then surprise us. There is a great story of a twelve year old who had this conversation with his father:

> "Why do we bury Granddad in such expensive clothes? It's a big waste of money."
> "Why is that?"
> "Because all the dirt will ruin them when he's buried."
> "We close the casket before we bury him."
> "Oh, I didn't know that."

What you can do:

- Be honest. Give as many details of the death as the child needs and wants. They're curious and interested. While a seven year old may be content with knowing that Grandpa's heart stopped, a twelve year old wants to know just what happened to the heart, how the hospital treated Grandpa, and who will fix things for Grandma now.
- Answer questions.
- Explain what feelings may come.
- Provide a journal for writing down feelings and thoughts, and writing letters to the person who died.
- Offer your love, understanding, and support.
- Involve your child as much as possible in planning the funeral or memorial service.

It was a good six months before Scott would talk about his sister. Her death was sudden and it seemed to shut him up. He didn't cry and he seemed afraid. Scott's mother sat down with him and told him she needed to talk. She said they were still a family, they would be there for each other, and it might help if he cried. She said some people cried best in the shower. Mom also said she loved Scott as much as she loved his sister and that they would always remember Jenny, even though they'd be sad a long, long time. All at once he said,

"Remember when Jen walked backwards to get the dog to drink from the lake and fell into the mud?" Scott and his mother began a "Remember When" session and laughed together, and the following week Mom noticed Scott taking much longer showers.

Teens

Teenage years themselves are a grief experience. It's the time of the loss of a childhood—no more cuddling into laps and getting read to and played with. It's not yet the reaching of adulthood, when you can make your own decisions and live your own life. It can be a very difficult time for everyone.

As a young woman I taught a lively, delightful Sunday School class of senior high students. At Christmas time I asked them to share their strongest Christmas memory. I thought they would say things like the year the tree fell over or when a first bike arrived. But no—one young man said, "The first year I didn't get any toys." Every head in the room nodded in agreement and I had a very clear memory of sitting on our staircase, wearing my new bathrobe and listening to my new clock radio. I was thirteen.

Teens can have added guilt at the time of a death because at this time of crisis they're starting to pull away from the family. They may feel scared and actually challenge death, something that is even more frightening to parents who have already buried one child. Boys may act very macho and refuse to cry or admit they have feelings. Girls may count heavily on their friends to listen to them and be supportive.

Our youth need and deserve our care and respect. They can't handle a death in the family all by themselves. They need our guidance. Their emotions are bubbling over anyway and they're watching their bodies change dramatically. One psychology teacher described it as "a massive running off of the hormones." It's a time of long talks with friends and real attempts to figure things out and understand life . . . and death. They may fantasize about their own deaths, much to the dismay of parents and other adults. We've seen teens sit together and count the number of people who would attend their funerals.

What you can do:

• Be honest.
• Tell about the death and give details.
• Explain what feelings may come.
• Encourage the youth to talk to a teacher, coach, or favorite relative if it's hard to open up to you.
• Say what you feel.
• Say what you need.

If you need your teen to be especially careful now, explain that you're afraid, too, and it will take a while to get back to normal.

• Touch, pat, hug. Give your love and understanding.
• Say it's okay to cry and it's okay for you to cry, too.
• Tell her how much you appreciate her.
• Respect his need for private time.

When Lonnie was murdered, his father said, "I was scared out of my wits for P.J. She was with a group of friends I didn't really know and she seemed so angry all the time." One night Dad asked P.J. if she wanted a hug. "No!" she said. Her father turned and started up the stairs. That was when P.J. called after him, "Dad, do you want a hug?" He did.

Give them time. Give them space. Give them your love. Children are wonderful people and great teachers. They deserve to know that death is a part of life and that in all parts of life someone will be there for them.

Several people believe that these concepts we've discussed stay with us all our lives, no matter how old we become. We all have magical thinking. We are all afraid at times. We all think our loved one will come back, even when we know it can't be so. Scratch us, any of us, and underneath you'll find a child.

Part Four

DEATH EDUCATION

8

EXPLAINING DEATH

W e've discussed some of the keys we need in teaching children what death is like. Paris realized the bee was different in death than in life, Randy understood that his brother would not be there anymore, and other children in our stories have asked questions and been given honest answers. When the questions come from young children, the answers can be simple:

• *What does it mean to be dead?*

"When someone dies, everything inside that person stops. The heart stops. The breathing stops. They don't eat or go to the bathroom anymore. The thinking and feeling stops, too. When a person is dead, that person cannot think about things. They cannot feel any hurt. It does not hurt to be dead. They cannot feel hot or cold. What is left is just the body; like a peanut shell without the peanut, like a schoolhouse without the children."

• *What does the body feel like?*

"The body feels cool, a lot like the cover of this book. You can touch the face on a doll if you want to. A doll's face feels a lot like a person feels when dead. The person will feel different and look different than when alive."

Explaining how the body will look is important, too. "Grandpa will have his eyes closed. He'll look as if he's asleep, but if you look closely you can tell he's not asleep. He's dead. When you sleep you breathe in and out, you turn over and sigh, all your inside parts are working away. When you've slept enough, you wake up. When a person is dead, that part that tossed and turned, laughed and cried is gone. Only the body is left. Grandpa will be wearing his suit. His hands will be folded. His glasses will be on his face, too, and he'll probably have a little bit of pink on his cheeks."

Then there are the other important things to explain:

The casket is a special box that holds the body. Often children are allowed to go with the family to select the casket and make funeral plans. It's also all right to allow the children to ask any questions they want about the casket, how it's sealed and balanced, why the feet may not show, or whether or not the person inside will be wearing shoes (probably the most common question we hear). They can touch the lining and push on the mattress and test the handles too.

At other times, the person may be buried in a plain pine box and wrapped in a special cloth called a shroud. The body returns to the gentle good earth no matter how it is buried.

Some people ask that their bodies be given to medical schools so young doctors can learn about the body and about illnesses. Still other people request to be cremated, that is, their bodies turned to ash. We'll talk more about these types of caring for the body in later Keys.

The funeral home is another important place to explain. The funeral home is a special place where we can go to say thank you and goodbye to the person who died. It is a big house (or building) and is very pretty inside. You'll see flowers and there will be people there to greet you and answer your questions. If at all possible, take your children to the funeral home for a separate viewing. (See Part Five.)

9

BURIAL

"There it goes," Andy said as he watched the casket containing his grandmother's body being lowered into the ground. "There it goes into the warm, soft ground."

For centuries that warm, soft ground has received the remains of those we love. And if we choose burial, someday that ground will welcome us as well. "What happens to the body?" is a leading question for all of us, especially children.

To explain burial, it's appropriate to say:

"We will go to a place called a cemetery. There will be chairs there and probably a tent top. There will be a hole in the ground called a "grave." The body will be in the beautiful box called a casket. The casket will go into the grave and be covered up with the warm, good earth. We can visit the grave whenever we want to."

Many cemeteries require a vault, and children need to know that this protects the body and helps the grave look nice. "A vault is a really big box. It is so solid and strong that water can't get in it. The ground can't sink in over it. This big box holds the casket where the body is."

It's also a good idea to describe the cemetery. Aunt Bess, whose story at age four began this book, used to say, "There are two committees. One goes around looking for the windiest, hottest hill in the county. That's where they put the cemetery. The second committee finds the coldest and windiest and that's where they build the college."

Sometimes families have a short service at the cemetery instead of a longer one at the funeral home. If this is the case, just telling the child what is likely to happen, who will probably be there, and what to expect can be very helpful. Oftentimes the child can take a flower from the service to dry and put in a special place or keep until it is ready to be thrown away.

Whether your family has a service in a funeral home, a church, or at the cemetery, you have had a chance to say goodbye and that is very important.

10

~~~~~~

CREMATION

Now that more and more people are being cremated, you're likely to need to explain cremation as well:

"When a body is cremated, the funeral director carefully wraps the body and takes it to a special place called a crematorium. The body is put into a special box. The box goes into a very small room, not like any room you have in your house. When the body is inside the room, the person taking care of the body goes out, carefully closing the door. That person pushes a little button. The button starts a very hot fire inside the little room and the fire changes the body. The body begins to gently melt into soft ashes. It's something like an ice cream cone that melts from the inside out. All that is left is the ashes. These go into a special machine that makes them smaller. Now the ashes look like ground-up seashells or very coarse sand.

"Finally, the ashes are put into a jar called an urn. Our family can do many nice things with the ashes. Some people scatter the ashes over a favorite place, some bury the urn or keep it in a special little house at the cemetery, and some people keep a tiny bit of the ashes in a locket or in a tiny box."

Remember John Chesnutt, who gave his children, Dara and Jefferson, a Mommy Box to keep after their mother died? John was also a great teacher when it came to cremation, in more ways than one. After we had talked about involving the children, he memorized the part in the book *Tell Me, Papa* about cremation. He went home, got Dara (age five) and sat her down under a big tree in their front yard. "Dara," he said, "Mommy has fought her cancer for a long, long time and her body can't fight anymore. She's going to die. Now, she'll always be our Mommy and we'll always be a family. We'll miss Mommy and we'll be sad for a long, long time, but we'll be all right." John took a deep breath.

"After Mommy dies," John went on, "there's this very nice man called a funeral director. You haven't met him yet. He'll carefully take Mommy's body to a special place with a special room. It's not like any room we have in our house. Inside the room is a very warm fire and that fire is so warm it gently melts Mommy's body like an ice cream cone would melt from the inside out. What's left is a fine ash and we'll put it in a really nice jar we pick out together. You may have more questions then. Now, do you want to go and say goodbye to Mommy?" Dara nodded. John stood up. Dara stood up. John started for the car and Dara didn't move.

"Dara?" John asked.

"What about Jefferson?" she replied.

"He's going to come with one of the grandmas," John explained.

Dara planted her feet firmly. "No," she said, looking Dad straight in the eye. "He should come with us." Children can be so smart!

John told us he did much better with Jefferson (age two). He explained how sick Mommy was and how she was going to die. He did the whole nine yards about saying goodbye, then looked at Dara. "Tell him about the body!" she exclaimed. John had this one down pat. "Jefferson, there's this very nice man called a funeral director. You haven't met him yet." John says, "I said it again . . . special room, special fire, not like any we have in our house, pretty jar called an urn, more questions later."

Then John said, "Picture if you will, this woeful scene. We are sitting at the hospital holding Bea's hand. I have a child on each knee and I am nothing but mush. We've said how much we love Mommy, we've thanked her for everything she did for us, for playing with us, for being such a great Mommy. Bea has said her goodbyes, too, and there's a touching moment of silence. We're all finished. Then I looked down at these big brown eyes and this pipey little five-year-old voice said, "Tell her about the body!"

John's last sentence in that part of the story was, "Mommy, there's this very nice man called a funeral director . . . you haven't met him yet."

That, in itself, is a touching, wonderful story of a child's acceptance, curiosity, and honesty. But John's story didn't end there. After the funeral, the funeral director called and said Bea's ashes were ready. John's mother asked if he wanted her to go get them. "No," John said, "the kids and I are going to do that."

They brought the ashes home. John got the beautiful blue-and-white ginger jar they had selected together. He put a plastic tablecloth over their family-room table and dumped the ashes from the funeral home onto the middle of the table. He gave each child and himself a tablespoon and spoonful by spoonful they put the ashes into the ginger jar, each time sharing a memory of Mommy. When all the ashes were in the jar, John put his hands over the hands of his children and together they sealed the jar. Dara looked up at her daddy and said, "This is so neat! Can I take this to show and tell?"

John showed creativity and tasteful courage in following his heart and involving his children in such a direct way. The dark shroud of death was removed and the only stop put on it all was that no, Dara didn't get to take the urn to show and tell.

There are, of course, other ways of caring for a body and those can be explained simply as well. Donating the body to science can be explained as a caring gift. The body is cared for with love and respect. Doctors and scientists study different parts to learn how to help people who are sick. After they have studied for a long time and learned all they can learn, the body is cremated and returned to the family.

You can talk about organ donation in much the same way. After a loved one dies, special doctors come in and gently take out everything that can be used by someone who is very, very sick. "I just told my daughters," Lucilla said, "that every part of their daddy that could help someone else was used. Some young person who has never had a strong heart has Daddy's strong heart now. A grandmama who couldn't see to bake cookies for her grandchildren has part of Daddy's clear eyes, and some mommy who couldn't go hiking with her kids has a new pair of lungs from Daddy." Today more and more organ recipients are meeting the families of the donors and building unique and special relationships.

If, on a rare occasion, a body is missing or not found, you can tell the child what you believe happened. You can also share your religious beliefs and say that no matter where the body is, you know that God (or Angels or Wonderful Friendly Spirits) guard it and love it and that no matter where it is, it is safe and not hurting anymore.

Lu's daughter was murdered. The killer was arrested and convicted of other killings, but Lisa's body was never recovered. She talked with Lisa's sister about her deep feeling. "Lisa loved the woods," she said. "I really feel in my heart that somewhere she is lying in a shallow grave in the midst of beautiful trees. Every day I imagine little squirrels chattering above her. I see deer walking over this sacred spot where she's buried." For Lu, this was comforting and, as it turned out, accurate. A hunter found her purse and later officials found her body buried in a place much as her mother had imagined it.

One of the tough questions you're likely to get, and to ask yourself, when a loved one is murdered is "Did he suffer?" Often for a child, this comes as "Was he scared?" Honest answers, because we really don't always know, are:

> "If he was, it was only for a very short time and then he was peaceful and not afraid at all."

> "I don't know for sure, but I do know that no matter how scared he might have been, it didn't last forever and all that time he knew we loved him very, very much."

Again, do your best in explaining how we care for the body and what happens. Listen for questions and let the children do what is comfortable for them. Remember, too, you don't have to do it all by yourself. If you don't have answers, call your funeral director or another professional who can help you find what you need to know.

This can be a rich, creative, satisfying experience for all of you, even if it is the saddest time in your life. In fact, you may be surprised at how much you learn from all this.

Part Five

THE FUNERAL

11

INVOLVING YOUR CHILD

After the questions about what dead is, what the body looks like, and what happens to the body of the person we love, we have that special time when we say "Thank you and goodbye" to our person. There will come a time, in everyone's life, when we take part in what one six year old called *Our own goodbye party and our long, sad parade*, the line of cars that slowly moves through the streets to the cemetery for the burial.

Funerals are those ceremonies that take place soon after death and at which there is often a body present.

Memorial services often do not have the body present and can be held any time and any place.

Open casket service enables visitors to see the body. The casket may be open throughout the funeral or closed just before the service starts.

Closed casket service has the body present in the casket but it cannot be seen or viewed.

The single most important thing to remember about a service is that if it is *your* family member, *you are in charge*. You can be as creative as you wish. The funeral director is there to facilitate and support your decisions.

Our nephew was murdered. He was the fourth generation in a Pennsylvania trucking firm. He loved trucks. He drove trucks. A big part of his life was around trucks and hard work. For most of the year, Steve wore flannel shirts. He was buried in his jeans and a flannel shirt. His children were involved in his service. Country-western music played at times. Even though he was dead, his personality was there at the service and he was still and always will be an important part of the family, wearing his flannel shirts in our memories.

We told a suicide survivor's group about Steve the trucker and one of the mothers present began to laugh. She made a date to take us to the cemetery where her son was buried because she said we would fully appreciate his grave marker. We met her at a nearby restaurant and followed her car as it wound through the cemetery. There was the headstone, sitting proudly on the hill with a beautifully engraved Peterbuilt truck below her son's name.

Eight months after Steve died, we visited his family in Pennsylvania and took a trip to the cemetery. There was the big, black headstone. Above his name was a carving of his favorite classic car. On the back of the stone was carved—you guessed it—a big semi-trailer truck. You can be as creative as you want.

Allowing your children to help plan and be part of a funeral may end up being one of your richest, most rewarding times. When my mother died, she was cremated. Her two teenage granddaughters helped with the arrangements and at the end of the service gave everyone a white carnation. They had set her napkin collection on two podiums. Every family member brought napkins for her collection whenever they traveled, and her nieces and nephews went through the scrapbooks holding the collection and remembered trips and good times. Her urn sat atop a beautiful crazy quilt Mother had made in 1919. The only regret I have is that we didn't play some harmonica music. As my cousin said, "Aunt Mary played a mean mouth harp." It would have been a fitting exit tune.

In the book *Animal Crackers*, young Bridget Marshall tells how her grandmother hid M&Ms and animals crackers whenever the family visited her. At Grandmother's funeral, Briget's father gave everyone a box of animal crackers which they opened and shared during the service.

One of the great joys in my career as a bereavement writer and lecturer is seeing and hearing the creative, healing things children have done at funerals. George Foley of York Casket Company tells of a family whose children each took one of Grandpa's tools to the funeral home to put in the casket with him. One placed the hammer by his hand, another his carpenter's plane, and another a favorite screwdriver.

For years George had saved toothpaste tube tops for a friend who built doll houses. It seems tops from toothpaste make perfect doll house lampshades. When this loving old builder died, George had handfuls of the tops left. He took them to the funeral home and together with his friend's granddaughter, Sarah, put all the tops in Grandpa's pockets.

We've seen a favorite coffee mug in a young mother's hands. We've seen beautiful paper-plate pictures in between dignified bouquets of flowers. Allowing children to draw pictures to put in the casket is an excellent way to say goodbye and express grief. Drawing on the center part of plain white paper plates turns the sides of the plates into neat frames.

In the very helpful book *Thank You for Coming to Say Goodbye*, by Janice L. Roberts and Joy Johnson, funeral director Dan Schaefer wrote a section titled "And then there's Jack": "Kim's children had done well with their first visit to their grandpa's viewing at my funeral home. They brought gifts, a small doll, and an action figure Tommy knew Grandpa would like. They wanted the bottom of the casket opened to make sure Grandpa's legs were there. In my experience, 80 percent of the children want this assurance. They counted the prayer cards and flowers, checked out the sealing mechanism on the casket, and things seemed to be going well. Then Kim said, 'Something's bothering them.' She asked and they replied, 'Why can't Jack say goodbye to Grandpa? He loved Grandpa and Grandpa loved him.' Jack was an 80-pound German Shepherd. We decided Jack should visit.

"The children walked Jack into the viewing room and together we helped them lift him up to see Grandpa. The children placed Jack's paw on Grandpa's arm. These children had done what was important. There are many children and adults who are not given the opportunity Jack was given. Let's hope books such as these can help make it easier to say goodbye."

12

FUNERAL DIRECTORS

No matter what your religious faith is, you're likely to be working with a funeral director. Thanks to creative innovators such as George Foley, whose casket group founded the York Children's Foundation, more and more funeral directors are aware of the needs of children and are adapting to the changing views regarding funerals and caring for grieving children.

As mentioned earlier, if you are planning a service for a family member or attending a visitation, the funeral director is there to facilitate and support. You can request such simple things as a small stool so children can climb up to the casket to see their loved one. This prevents aching arms from holding the child each time she wants to take a peek. On a larger scale you can:

• *Take the children with you if you are planning the service.*
Rob's father died when he was in college. When he arrived home, he asked his mother about the funeral and when he could see his dad. She told him she had already had his father cremated to "save" him the grief involved. It was years later that Rob was finally able to tell his mother how angry he was not to be included. Rob is not the first child to be wrongly "protected." We have listened to fifty year olds who lamented the fact they were not allowed to attend a funeral and say goodbye.

Loren told us, "When I was ten or twelve, my grand-mother died. She had been in our house, and actually she died there, for a long time. Every afternoon after school I read to her, I took her trays up, I climbed on her bed and talked with her. I even cleaned her up after a bowel accident once, for God's sake! And after she died, my mother wouldn't let me go to the funeral. It was ridiculous. I have resented it most of my life."

Teens are often not only eager to be involved, but also tremendously creative. We've seen football uniforms worn when youths attended as a team. There has been scuba diving equipment, favorite T-shirts, school annuals, and much more draped over chairs and podiums. Poems have been read and songs have been sung by wonderful, caring teens, many of whom had their own visitation program and their own memorial service at the school.

• *Request a child's visitation*
Some funeral homes invite children to come an hour before the regular visitation or the service for a visitation program. They and any parents who wish to attend sit together on the floor while a funeral director explains exactly how the body is cared for and what the body *and* the viewing room look like. Children are invited to ask questions, are shown pictures of the embalming room and viewing rooms, and are then invited to view the body. Janice Roberts, who created one of the first children's viewings, says, "I have never had a child who didn't want to view the body. They have good questions and in many ways they deal with death and funerals better than many adults." There is nothing a funeral director does that cannot be lovingly and caringly explained to children.

Children can share memories during their visitation session. They can draw pictures to put in the casket and write letters to be gently placed in a pocket or in the loved one's hand. Special objects can be brought at this time as well.

While older children in our earlier story brought Grandpa's tools to put in the casket, Lacie had a different plan. When she attended the children's visitation for her baby sister, who had died of sudden infant death syndrome, she carefully carried in the baby's mobile that was over her sister's crib. During her visitation, the funeral director helped her put it over the bassinet that held her sister's tiny body.

13

WHEN A CHILD CAN'T ATTEND

Needless to say, if children do not want to view the body or attend the funeral they should not be forced to do so. Funeral director Dan Schaefer has an answer to the question *Should my child attend the funeral?* It's a strong *Never! Unless he's prepared first.* We've told how to describe the body, the viewing room, the funeral home. Letting the child know that people will be crying and laughing and sharing memories of the dead person helps, too.

When after you explain and prepare, your child still does not want to see the body or go to the service, there are other things you can do:

• *Take pictures*

In Victorian times and actually until fairly recently, it was common practice to photograph the body in the casket. Pictures were sent to relatives too far away to attend the service. The photos often arrived in an envelope bordered in black, telling the family that either a death had occurred or that the service had been held. Take pictures of the body, the flowers, the people who are gathered. If your child asks questions later, you can share these. Many families are now videotaping the services.

• *Give the details*

Telling your child what the service was like can be important.

When Jarel's father died, her 12-year-old son was determined not to attend his grandfather's funeral, saying over and over that he'd never really known him very well because they'd lived so far away. On the drive home, a week after the service, Jarel talked about what happened at the service, what people had said, and how her father had looked. She laughed and shared two jokes a cousin had told her. Her son didn't comment or respond. Jarel rambled on, laughing at some of her own memories of her dad. They had no sooner arrived home that she overheard her son giving detail after detail of her memories and the service to their next-door neighbor.

Even if your child doesn't act eager to hear the details or see the pictures, you've included her in this important event in your family's life.

• *Make sure young children have a safe place to stay*
When a child doesn't want to attend a service, we need to be careful not to give a guilt message. Make sure the children know it's all right not to be there, that you will tell them all about it later. The person watching them needs to know that it's perfectly fine for them not to be present at the funeral and that they can enjoy this time as well. You can always leave paper and markers for them to draw a picture about what they think the funeral is like or to be put in a special box later on.

Remember, children need to be involved and included in some way in this event, which has an impact on and changes your family. Whether he helps you decide that Grandma would look better in a casket lined with pink or that Dad's ashes should be scattered in the lake where he loved to fish, or you sit with the child after the fact and share who was there and what the service was like, you've told him he is important. His opinion matters. You value his feelings and needs.

14

OTHER PEOPLE

U nfortunately, you are likely to be pressured by some family and friends to "protect" your child by not allowing her to attend or become involved. If your child wants to take part, stand firm. Grief and funerals are family affairs and it will be *you*, not the other people, who will some day have to explain why your child was not invited to be part of the family at this important time.

Lori's mother was adamant that Lori's children not attend their uncle's funeral. It wasn't "good" for them. They'd "be in the way." After a long time, Lori gave in. Even though the children wanted to go, they stayed with a baby-sitter. They were picked up after the service. Nothing was said. A week later, the three year old began acting out by disobeying, throwing heavy objects, and yelling at his mother. His seven-year-old sister reverted to bed-wetting and what Lori described as "crying jags." As Lori was driving by the cemetery one day, her little boy said, "That's where Uncle Gene is. We can't see him because we're bad." Lori drove into the cemetery, took her children by the hand, and walked to her brother's grave. "You aren't bad!" she said. "Sometimes grown-ups make mistakes. I made a mistake when I didn't take you to the funeral. We're going to change that right now!" A special trip was made to the funeral home and the party store. After the funeral director talked to the children, they bought balloons and a magic marker. Each child wrote, or at age three dictated, a message to Uncle Gene. They took the balloons and some dandelions they had picked to the grave and had their own goodbye session with their uncle. Bed-wetting and acting out stopped. The next Sunday Lori brought her family to the grave along with a picnic basket filled with hot dogs and potato salad.

People who love us and care for us have good intentions. They don't want the children to hurt and don't realize that children may well hurt more if they are denied knowledge and opportunities. This is the time when you may have to say, "I know you mean well, but I'm the parent and I have to follow my own intuition and my own knowledge in this matter."

It's also a good idea to realize that grief breeds anger in almost any family. I can remember my mother talking about my Aunt Doris after Doris's husband died. Over and over Mom would say, "That's just not like Doris. That's just not like Doris." No matter how often I intelligently and repeatedly told my mother that after a death families get angry and this was normal even for this lovely, gentle lady I called Aunt Doe, she just looked at me and said, "That's just not like Doris." Anger comes like spring rain and autumn winds when we grieve, so if you insist on involving your children and explaining death and grief to them, be ready for some angry talk. Don't take it personally and don't get hooked by it. Love the person who is angry, know he or she has good intentions, then follow your heart and your head.

Part Six

GRIEF EDUCATION

15

YOUR OWN GRIEF
PATTERNS

*G*rief is the multitude of emotions that come when we experience a significant loss. *Mourning* is the expression of that grief. Both are family affairs. Both will be determined to some degree by how all the generations of your family have dealt with grief and the manner in which they mourned.

Since most of our hesitancy and concern in teaching children the keys to learning about death and grief comes from our own backgrounds and, especially, our own fears, it's fitting and right to take a look at what holds us back and how we can change for the better.

While Aunt Bess, who appeared on the first pages of this book, was a gutsy, curious four year old, she was also a member of a large family of wailers. You may have read about some cultures that have a custom of families hiring professional wailers to follow the funeral procession. The richer the family, the more wailers appeared and, of course, the louder they wailed.

The cultural norm in our family was to carry a handful of cotton handkerchiefs and cry loudly at the funeral. At the house it was different. We laughed and told stories and watched television, but once we left the house for the church, we changed. We wailed.

You received messages about how to grieve and they will affect how you teach your children and what new keys you adopt for your own grief and what old and new keys you give your children. To help get a picture or history of how you grieve and what you want to change in your grief patterns, you may want to write down:

• *Your first experience with death and grief.*

I have a very vague memory of my father holding me as my grandfather's body was carried from his home. I remember my mother and grandmother standing by an old cookstove. They were crying. My daddy was holding me close. I was afraid. I didn't go to the funeral. I wasn't told anything. It took me years to not have a first feeling of *fear* when anyone even mentioned death.

How did you learn about this first death? Was it a person or a pet? What were you told? Were you protected or included? What will you teach your children that is the same and what will be different?

• *Your first viewing of a body.*

Because of my fear reaction, I passed up a real opportunity to grow. A friend of mine died while we were in high school. The funeral was held in the church across the alley from my house. Mother asked if I wanted to go and I said, "No. I didn't know him that well." Big lie! I put on my bathing suit and spent the entire time in the backyard washing my dad's car. Tears poured down my cheeks as I heard the music from the church. The noise of the hose drowned my sobs. I was afraid of seeing the body. I didn't want people to see me cry.

Years ago some families required children to kiss the body. We've since found that the actual number was exaggerated, as were many of the stories around the event. There's nothing right or wrong about kissing the cheek or hand of a dead loved one. It all depends on how you feel and what you want to do. Remember, the body will feel a lot like the cover of this book. There has been a tremendous surge of relief as parents were allowed and encouraged to hold their stillborn babies. We've seen big brothers and sisters ages four to twelve hold the babies as well. I will never forget reading of a mother walking down the hall of a hospital, carefully and firmly holding the hand of her child, who was covered and lifeless on the gurney being pushed tenderly by a nurse whose cheeks were covered with tears. The fears and taboos against touching the body date back to times of rampant disease, poor burial practices, and scary stories by the fireside. Today we know it's a personal choice, and whatever you decide is all right for you.

To discover your own bereavement pattern, ask yourself: Were you made to look at the body or told not to peek? Were you told what you would see? Did you hear ghost stories or other scary stories about bodies suddenly sitting up in the casket? Of people being buried alive? Of children being forced to kiss the corpse? Personally, I still love scary stories and I still whistle when I walk by a cemetery alone, which leads us to the next question.

• *What were your family superstitions?*

I was told that if a bat or bird got in your house, someone would die. I was told that when the barn owl hooted, someone would die, and there are very few of us out there who haven't jumped down the sidewalk saying, "Step on a crack and you'll break your mother's back." As I was writing the first draft of this paragraph, we were on a working vacation in Maine. Our house-sitter in Omaha called to tell us she had walked in one day to find a pigeon perched nonchalantly on one of our antique clocks. Big bird! We can look back and smile, but these ideas go deep into our subconscious and affect us for years. Just ask any sixth-generation Irish family who has a banshee in their background. We can still have that tinge of fear before our rational side takes over. It's a lot like the immediate feeling of guilt that comes when a loved one dies, even if we haven't done anything to deserve it.

Did your family have superstitions around death? Did anyone ever say to you, "Don't do that! Something bad will happen to you!"? What old messages hang on around the mystery of death? How do you feel when you think of them?

- *How did you show your feelings?*
Because of the wailing tradition, I thought my job was to be strong and not be a bother to the adults. I wasn't to cry. That's why my father's car was so clean after my friend's funeral. The manner in which you've been allowed to share your feelings will determine to a great extent how you accept your children's grief. It's not unusual for us to have to reparent ourselves, to give ourselves permission to cry or permission to be comforted. Looking back can help us all make some of the changes that lead us to wholeness.

Were you allowed to cry? Were you scolded or reprimanded for your feelings? Were you told "not to be _____"? (fill in your own blanks). And were you left to fend for yourself and find answers wherever you could?

Looking at how we've been taught to grieve gives us the option to change anything that holds us back or harms us and preserve and pass on to the next generation those customs and teachings that help us move through our grief in healthy, healing ways. We can grow. We can change. We can even find it enjoyable.

16

THE JOY OF GROWTH AND CHANGE

We all grow up in family systems with tribal rules. Some families have tribal rules saying, "You never, never laugh around someone who is sad." Or, "As soon as someone you know dies, take a casserole to the house—preferably tuna." Or, and an especially harmful one, "Don't talk about the person who died. It will make the (spouse, son, daughter, parent) sad." And the most harmful one of all, "Don't talk about it to the children; they're too young to understand."

When you decide to be a grief companion, to go with a child on a journey of sorrow, you walk into a rich, colorful, honest world. When you tell your family you are taking the children to the funeral home, teaching them what the funeral director does, reading to them books about death and grief, and allowing them to ask absolutely any question that pops into their heads, be ready for resistance:

"How can you do such a thing?"

"What are you thinking of?"

"Be careful! You're no expert!"

—and my mother's favorite, "What will *they* think?"

I never figured out who *they* were, but they certainly had a powerful influence on Mother's life.

These are some of the most common responses to any sort of change and growth. The system, the tribe, will do everything they can to get you back to a place where they are more comfortable. Ever lost a lot of weight? Chances are you received candy as a gift at one time or another.

When my husband and I first went into counseling careers, a new concept hit the streets and the literature. *Transactional analysis* challenged some of the old Freudian ideas and let a fresh wind blow over the world of psychology. It let us take a look at ourselves and help ourselves improve, grow, and change and have fun at the same time. Transactional analysis, or T.A. as it became known, tells us we have three parts, parts that make us look like a snowman.

The top (snowman head) is labeled *Parent.*

The middle part is labeled *Adult.*

And the bottom is labeled *Child.*

There are statements common to each part. "Don't you dare teach that child about death! It will scare her" comes directly from the Parent part. You can almost see that finger pointing at you and waggling. Scolding, demanding, judgmental. The Parent part is also nurturing and loving. "Of course you can ask me any question about death and dying. I love you and I'm here to help." We are critical and nurturing—parents, one and all.

You read, you ask questions, then say to yourself, "Perhaps it would be valuable to teach children about death. Death is a part of life and knowing about it will alleviate fears and allow them to ask questions." Very adult, right? Intellectual. Fact-finding. Nonfeeling. Sensible. The middle part of the snowman is the Adult.

And that Child in all of us says, "Gee whiz! This stuff is fascinating! Plus I have permission to cry and play with the kids and ask some questions myself. Right on!" The voice gets a little higher pitched. The eyes get bright and wider. There's a smile. The Child. It's the Child in all of us who cries and laughs and sneaks a peek at the body when no one is looking. The Child is the delightful, learning, growing part of us.

In teaching children about death and grief, you will pull on all three parts. Your loving Adult can counteract that scolding, worried part (of yourself and others) and say, "Children really need this chance to say goodbye." Your Adult can go out and get the resources necessary and the Child part of you can share feelings and give information in a way that a four year old will appreciate and understand.

One of the most important tasks or jobs of the Adult part is to keep our Parent part from beating up on the Child in us. The next time you're feeling guilty, you probably have some Critical Parent part pounding away on the little kid inside. That's time to bring out the Adult and say, "Excuse me," (the Adult is always polite) "but I do not deserve to feel guilty about not visiting my mother more often before she died." Guilt is unproductive and stress inducing. We can find productive ways to deal with this feeling, such as a letter to Mother telling her I'm sorry. She would understand. (Apologies can come from any part.)

If you go to the children, armed with adult reasoning and nurturing parent statements, arms around a load of books on grieving children and videos such as *Children Grieve, Too* and *Thank You for Coming to Say Goodbye*, and still feel the resistance is too much for you, compromise:

- Read the books to the children who are interested.
- Leave them around for adults to find and read.

- Visit with the funeral director about talking to the ch.
  when you get to the funeral home, church, or synagogue
- Back off some, but don't give up. Do everything you can to
  teach and reach them. Let them know you're not afraid to
  listen to them and to answer their questions.

As you read the books, look at your own grief patterns
and picture yourself teaching your children what you would
have liked to have been taught. You'll find a lot of your old
fears turning into new excitement. As one father said, "Hey!
This is a really interesting time! All at once the kids feel
they're a real part of this family. They're asking hundreds of
questions and saying some really neat things, and for the first
time ever, we're actually *listening* to each other." Which
leads us to another area. You may be surprised at the response you get from children who know you are there for
them.

17

YOU DON'T HAVE TO DO IT ALL YOURSELF

Whether it's asking a funeral director, clergy person, or bereavement counselor how to involve your particular children in a funeral service or spotting potential problems in a grieving child, it's vital that you know you don't have to shoulder the entire burden yourself. Your funeral director can tell you how to get in touch with experts through organizations such as The Compassionate Friends, Association for Death Education and Counseling, and the American Academy of Bereavement.

As one of our children said after we had blended two families of three children each, "One thing about a family this size, there's always at least one person who doesn't think you're crazy." When you start talking about asking what the children think, guiding them through grief, and answering their questions, you may be surprised at who surfaces to support you from your own family.

You don't have to do it all alone. There are school counselors to help you and bereavement counselors to consult with you. In almost every community in America now, there is a hospice or support group. In one of those organizations there will be someone who will fit the bill, answer your questions, and fill your needs.

Part Seven

GRIEF EDUCATION FOR CHILDREN

We cannot lose anything or anybody without experiencing a multitude of feelings or emotions. Children have many if not all of the feelings adults experience, but on a somewhat different timetable and in a more concrete way. Knowing that the explosion of real and honest feelings is normal can help you recognize that the child is not being "bad" or "naughty." The child is grieving. In order to teach and guide children through grief you need to know what may or may not happen.

18

SADNESS AND
DEPRESSION

Sadness is that depth of sorrow that brings tears to our eyes, sobs to our throats, and is easy to identify. After four-year-old Noah's daddy died, he ran up to his grandfather, crying every step of the way. He climbed onto Granddad's lap, looked up through his tears, and said, "You know what this is, Granddad? This is *Sad, Sad, Sad!*" No one could have described it better.

Depression, on the other hand, is that creeping feeling of shadow that sneaks up on us and is difficult to put into words or describe. We feel "blue," or it's a "gray" time. We feel "down," "immobilized." We don't know what to do or how to enjoy life. You know the feeling.

Children can feel depressed, too. Maddie wasn't quite three when her favorite person, her grandfather, who she called Buddy, died. Her Buddy was dead. Her mother found her one afternoon after her naptime, sitting in a corner of her room, facing the wall. "What's the matter, Maddie?" Mommy asked, sitting down on her daughter's bed and patting the space beside her. Maddie stood up, sighed, and went to her toy shelf. Picking up a sad-eyed, floppy, stuffed dog, she took it to her mother, put it on the bed beside her, and said, "Buddy gone." She patted the floppy dog. "Maddie," she said softly. "Maddie." She felt like a sad-eyed, floppy dog with nothing inside. She felt depressed.

The key to teaching about this feeling we have all known is to add some cuddling and hugs. Tell the child it is okay to feel sad and down, that you feel or have felt that way, too. Like all feelings, it will go away after awhile. Talking and crying are wonderful ways to begin healing. We all, no matter what age, need a good cry now and then. After a good cry it can help to do something with your child, such as a short walk, a trip to the store, some exercise that gets us moving.

19

ANGER AND ACTING OUT

Our entire world changes when someone we love and need is suddenly gone. When we're not sure about anything anymore, it's natural and appropriate to get mad. Anger is truly one of the most misunderstood reactions to death.

Children may be angry at many things and people. They may feel anger toward:

- parents
    for not telling them Grandma was so sick
    for not protecting them or the person who died
    for spending so much time with the sick person or, now, with other family members, friends, and professionals such as funeral directors, lawyers, and others

- those others who
    didn't make their loved one well
    killed their person (drunk drivers, murderers)

- the person who died
    for leaving them and the family
    for not taking care of himself or getting into danger
    for not saying goodbye
    for causing all this upset and sorrow

• sisters and brothers
  for getting more attention
  for grieving at a different pace or with different feelings
  just because they're handy and available

Children can be angry at themselves as well. They may wish they had done something different, said something they didn't say, been kinder and loved better.

Anger will go someplace. It has to get out. Some children may act out with behavior parents haven't seen for years.

Marissa thought her son Gabe was headed for trouble the rest of his life. After his father died, he turned his little brother into a punching bag. No matter how much she talked to him, scolded, gave him time outs, and finally spanked him, Gabe would wait until she wasn't looking and punch his brother on the arm or in the back.

Marissa enrolled Gabe in a program at a nearby center for grieving children where an entire group of kids talked about how angry they were at their parent, sibling, or grandparent who had died. Gabe spent more than two hours in the Emotion Commotion room, hitting the walls with soft, fuzzy balls, jumping onto bean bags, and punching a real punching bag. Marissa was able to gain insights into how her family could express anger in healthy ways, and after two sessions Gabe apologized to his little brother, talked more with his mom, and started on the road to healing.

The key here is to get the anger out in ways that don't hurt someone else or the child. Explaining that anger is normal when someone dies and that we have to use it in healthy ways comes first and as soon as you see the child is angry.

We've mentioned several ways to express anger: writing it out, running it out, hitting a bed with a dish cloth, pounding a pillow, and, for older children, participating in a fast game of basketball or tennis or other vigorous sport. As always, talking it over with a person we trust is the single most important thing we can do.

20

‹‹‹

GUILT AND RESPONSIBILITY

D an Schaefer, in his excellent book *How Do We Tell the Children?* talks about guilt and responsibility going hand-in-hand. Children can feel guilty about what they did do, didn't do, or thought about the person who died. They can also feel guilty about how they are grieving and how their actions are affecting their family in this time of sadness. If a sibling or close friend near their own age dies, they can have what we call survivor's guilt: *Why her and not me?* This is especially prominent if someone dies in an accident.

They can also have a sense of responsibility:

"Mom always said I'd be the death of her. Now she's dead."
"If I had just prayed harder he would have lived."
"I got mad and said I wished he was dead . . . now he is."

Be sure a child understands exactly why a person died. If the person was murdered, be sure the child knows it was the killer and not the child who caused the death.

Actual Responsibility
I was about ten when a high school sophomore in my hometown was asked to move her father's car to make more room for tables during a family reunion. Her foot hit the gas pedal instead of the brake. The car pinned her father against a tree, killing him. I spent hours in my bed at night trying to

realize how that must feel for her. I was, and still am, tremendously sorry for her grief and how guilty she must have felt. It's one of the horrible "if only" times we've all known.

And when another high school friend, whose red hair and freckles were a constant delight to everyone, saw me on the street 20 years later, we just stared at each other and then began to hug and cry. Her two teenage boys were speeding when their truck hit the van driven by my cousin. Her sons were killed, my cousin was decapitated, and her baby riding with her died as well. We were all victims. We were all severely traumatized.

There is not a one of us who hasn't stopped dead in our tracks while the media played a tape of a 911 call where the frantic voice of a young boy sobs that he shot his sister. "Oh, don't die! Oh, don't die!" I remember hearing in one such call.

When this worst-case scenario plays out, professional help is needed. Self-forgiveness and family forgiveness is essential to heal these scars. Forgiveness from the person who died needs to be felt and believed. This is when the search for a bereavement counselor who knows a lot about empathy is priority one.

In addition to being sure you find a good bereavement counselor, understanding and love is in order. Over and over one mother said to her daughter who accidentally killed her brother, "I know you did not mean to do this! I know you would have done anything to take that one second back. And what I want you to know is I love you and I will be here for you through our tears and all our awful, awful feelings." Her mother also told her, very sincerely, that if she could change places with her, she would.

Part Eight

~~~~~~

FEARS AND WORRIES

A ll at once it isn't just a scary story or a spooky movie. It's real. We all become frightened when death occurs. When we cleaned out Marv's mother's house after she died, our sister-in-law looked at the empty rooms and said, "I knew this was coming and I've been so afraid of it." We, those children of years ago, were now the family seniors. We were orphans—all our parents were dead now and not a one of us was younger than 50, yet all those childhood fears rumbled around inside us. Our parents weren't there to protect us anymore. Our safe and secure world was gone. Who would be next to die?

If we're thinking that in middle age, imagine how much more traumatic and intense it must be for a six year old. Death is frightening. Change is scary.

21

~~~~~~

WORRY QUESTIONS

There are several common concerns heard from children. In reality, they're pretty much the same questions we hear from ourselves and other adults.

• *What's going to happen to me?*

This is a very sensible question. If Mom has died, leaving a seven-year-old daughter, who will make breakfast and pack her lunch? What about picking out school clothes? It all translates into "Who will take care of me now?" In many ways it's a similar fear and worry to that which my mother felt when my dad died. Mother was sixty and had grown up in an age when women didn't work outside the home and her entire job was being a homemaker for my father and me. She didn't know how to change an electrical fuse or water the yard. Sure, she learned and she learned fast, but her words when her husband died were, "Why does this happen just when I need someone?"

My Aunt Dorothy died when I was twenty. Her husband was at her bedside 100 miles away. Their ten-year-old son, Ron, was staying with my parents. I had come home for the weekend and found Mother, Dad, and another couple who were close friends sitting at the kitchen table holding hands and clutching handkerchiefs. "Aunt Dorothy is just about gone," my mother said. I was still young enough to feel like a kid in this situation and my first response was, "Where's Ron?"

I found him upstairs in my old bedroom, almost hidden under the covers of the old iron bed, shivering. That was 40 years ago and I don't remember how I started our conversation or what all we talked about, but I do remember the two of us counting the number of people in our family who would take care of either one of us if we really needed it. I do remember him sitting up in the bed and listing people and I do remember saying we wouldn't be this afraid and worried forever. I didn't know anything about death and grief then, but it goes to show that we can trust our intuition and that talking really does help.

Children see family members crying who always before were happy and laughing. Their home becomes chaotic with people coming and going and bringing food. As family arrives, sleeping arrangements change. Children overhear conversations and often get only part of what is being said, adding to their imagination and fears.

Dorothy Ferguson, author of *Little Footprints* and *A Bunch of Balloons*, talks about hearing people talk after her father died. Over and over she heard, "The poor little ones," and all at once realized she was one of those "poor little ones." It was a long time before her mother convinced her she would be cared for and loved and part of a family.

• *What will happen next?*
Here's another common fear. I will bet you that if you're like my family, someone, in the midst of a church women's delicious funeral lunch will casually say, "Well, everything comes in threes. I wonder what will happen next." The old superstitions pop up and children's eyes tend to dart around the tables wondering if the whatever is going to happen to them.

When drastic change happens we tend to brace ourselves and get ready for whatever is next. Change really does promote change and there can be a lot "happening next."

More than once we've seen families move because half or all of the income has died along with the breadwinner. An article in our local newspaper told of a school program to help young students at risk. The program was designed to raise grades of those students who had a pattern of falling behind. The writer told of Jeremy, who was falling behind in his school work. Then, almost as an afterthought, the article mentioned the following:

> Jeremy was eight.
> His mother had abandoned him.
> His grandmother had taken him in to live with her.
> Three months later, his grandmother died.
> An aunt traveled 300 miles to bring him to Omaha.
> He moved into a new home in a new city with relatives he hardly knew.

Not once did anyone pick up that Jeremy was grieving multiple griefs. No wonder his schoolwork was slipping. That was the least of his worries!

Jeremy needed to be told over and over by many people that there would always be someone there for him, that no matter what happened he was precious and valuable and lovable. Jeremy needed support and help so he could build a courage muscle that would help him endure, because with Jeremy, like so many others, "it ain't over yet."

- *Will anyone else die?*
  After a friend of my father's died suddenly, I was terrified that my dad would die, too. It's a shock, that first realization that people die, and it takes some getting used to. I waited for Dad to come home every afternoon. I worried when he drove the car. This question is one with only one answer: *Yes.* Others will die. My father lived 12 years more after

my fears at age nine, but like everyone else in the whole world, he died. He was sixty-three and I was twenty-two.

It is horrific when a family is involved in an accident or an illness where more than one person dies. A friend was in the hospital with a new baby when her husband and two of her three other daughters were killed in an auto accident. Is it any wonder the surviving little girl whispered to her mother, "Who's next, Mommy? Who's next?" It was the same question pounding up against the mother's heart.

Usually, however, we can say to the child who has this question, "not for a long time." Mothers have often said, "I'm very healthy and very much alive. I'm going to be a grandmother to your little children and live to be very, very old." And usually, they do.

• *Am I going to die?*

We often act as if death is catching. Children are not allowed to go to the home of a child whose father has died. We keep them from funerals. We act as if death were waiting around the corner to grab us.

Many times this first death in a child's life brings the startling realization that everyone and everything dies at some time . . . and that means me, too. Very often children whose baby brother or sister die voice this fear. Preschoolers try hard to make the connection and make sense of things that frequently elude adult observations as well. If one baby dies, why not me? Or, why didn't I die?

Here's where we can tell the child how healthy she is, how most times when we get sick, we get well again right away. "Aunt Lu's heart was very, very sick. All the doctors and all the medicine couldn't fix it. Your heart is strong and healthy and good," one mother told her five year old after his aunt died from a heart infection. Then she put his hand on his chest until he felt his heartbeat. "Hear that?" she asked, "Just feel that strong heart beating away. You and I and Daddy will live a long, long time. Just listen to this!" and she held his hand over her own heart.

Of course, there is always the exception when no matter how hard we try to stay healthy and live all those long years we promised, we die. If within a short time of reassuring your child you will be old, gray, and in the rocking chair you're diagnosed with a terminal illness, that's the time to renegotiate, to go into counseling, and to make arrangements so the child will know there will be a loving adult around to care for her. And again, be honest. "Yes, we do expect to live for years and years and years. And if that doesn't happen, we'll see to it that you're all right and that there will always be someone there for you and to take care of you until you grow up."

• *How will my friends act?*

This isn't just a child's concern. Often after the death of a child, parents tell us they find out who their real friends are. As we mentioned, some people act as if death is catching and friendships are affected. Here is when talking to the child's teacher, perhaps asking her to come to your home, can be helpful. If the child can be present as you and the teacher visit, fears can be expressed and the child will know there's a friendly face waiting on that first day back to school. At other times, children know their friends pretty well, and returning to school can be a tremendous relief for them.

There will be questions and fears not mentioned here. Keep in mind that no matter how well you do, how hard you study, how often you consult with experts you'll miss something now and then. A pediatric oncology nurse told of two little girls who were friends because both had cancer and were undergoing chemotherapy. Unexpectedly, one died. The other little girl's mother drove to Karen's office immediately. They prepared for how Shari would be told about this death, what her questions would be. They even role-played the whole event. Mom drove home, fully prepared. She took Shari on her lap and said, "Shari, I have some very sad news. Becky died last night." Shari looked at her for a second, then said, "Geez. What did they do with her toys?" No one had thought of that question. While it makes us smile a tender smile, it also shows the concerns children have. One of the things some terminally ill little girls do is "will" their Barbie doll collections to friends or little sisters.

22

DEACTIVATING YOUR OWN FEARS

We can become paralyzed with fear. How often do we start our sentences with "Yes, but if I do that I'm afraid . . ."? We're afraid to talk to our children because they might become upset. We're afraid of what people will think of us. We're afraid we'll do something wrong—say the wrong thing, think the wrong way, grieve the wrong way.

"I don't think I'm doing this grief thing right," a widow told a friend. "I think I should feel worse."

A teenage boy was especially frightened about attending the funeral of a friend's father. He rehearsed and rehearsed going up to his friend, shaking his hand, and saying something nice. He had heard the word "condolences" used and liked it. He said it over and over, yet when he hugged his friend, he said, "Congratulations." The friend never heard him. He heard and felt the hug and the intent of sympathy and care.

Our fears often seem like a thundering herd of elephants, but when we really look at them, they turn into mice with microphones. When you yourself are afraid of dealing with the fears of your children, try this:

- Make a list of all your fears, no matter how small, no matter how big.

- Cross out the ones that you see are unfounded. (*I'm afraid I'll never stop crying.* You will. *I'm afraid of learning new skills at this point in my life.* You can.)
- Now take the surviving fears. Draw a line down the center of your paper. On one side list your real fears. On the other side list options you have. (*I'm afraid I'll lose the house.* Option: move to a smaller apartment, look for a better job, hang on as long as I can, etc.)

Once you get your own fears down on paper and under control, you'll be more comfortable facing the fears of your children. This whole book is about grief, and grief doesn't last forever. Neither will your fears and your feelings.

Part Nine

^^^

WHAT TO EXPECT

So much has changed. So much is new. It's difficult to anticipate what may happen next. There are many behaviors and feelings in children that can be troublesome unless we know they may be coming our way. And just as they occur in children, you'll probably be able to recognize many of them in yourself when you're grieving.

So many of us feel uncomfortable around sadness and mourning that we want people to "get better" so we'll feel better. We ignore the behaviors and the feelings. We push them aside. We pretend they're not there. But like the weather, they're there all right; and once we know they're normal and an active, often healing part of grief, they aren't quite as frightening.

23

DENIAL AND BLOCKING

One of the truly classic books about children and grief is Helen Fitzgerald's *The Grieving Child*. Helen says children can use their vivid, active imaginations to block out that which is unpleasant and hurtful. How many times have you totally forgotten to do something you really didn't want to do? We can still block out the unpleasant as adults.

Death and grief can be overwhelming. We become numb. I feel as if I'm encased in plastic when it happens to me. Children deal with this feeling by imagining it away; and sometimes adults do the same. For years after my Uncle Truman died, his daughter imagined him getting up every morning, packing his lunch pail, and going to work. She was thirty.

It's difficult for children to understand the finality of death, just as it's hard for me not to expect my father to be sitting on the front porch when I drive by my old house. In our culture, we fix things, we replace things, we get newer and better; but we can't fix or replace or get a newer and better sister when that sister dies. We can, however, repair broken hearts and give children new ideas and information.

I mentioned my mother saying that Aunt Dorothy was "just about gone." Our language can encourage the denial: "We'll see her soon." "She is not dead, just gone away." "He's gone to his reward (home—rest—whatever)."

It's normal to have trouble comprehending death. As one mother said, "Shock is a blessing. Without it our hearts would break for sure." More than one parent has hurried down a street because she was certain her dead daughter had just turned the corner. We *see* the people we love who have died. We *hear* the voice. We *know* when the phone rings it's them. Luckily, it takes a while for it to sink in and to know they are never coming back. Can we expect less from a child?

If denial or blocking goes on for a long time and you become concerned, talk to your child. Talking is always your first move, your first recourse. Ask how he learned about the death. Helen Fitzgerald mentions a little boy who drew her a picture of his mother sitting by him on his bed and labeled it "Mom Telling Me About Dad's Death." As he was leaving, he turned to Helen and said, "That's not really how I found out. I knew before Mom told me. I heard our maid on the telephone."

Be gentle. Be firm. Be honest when you tell your child once again that the person she loved is dead and never coming back. You can talk about having memories, of that person always living in your hearts, and you can talk about how it takes a long time to realize you'll never see them again except in your mind's eye. And equally important, you can encourage your child to talk as well . . . and to draw and sculpt and do all the other things we'll mention when we talk about ways to cope.

24

REGRESSION

As we said, it's the child in all of us that grieves. It's the child in us that cries and fears and needs to cling. "I'm just going to go home, lay down, and suck my thumb!" said one of our coworkers after a really hard day. Sleep in a fetal position? I do. When we are hit with a tragedy, we all regress or "go back" to a position or time or place or behavior where we feel safe. Worried? Our friend Jim curls his hair like he did when he was nine. One daughter bites her nails. And I'll confess—the only time I get really hungry for a frosted chocolate brownie with nuts is when I'm anxious about something. Whether we suck a thumb, bite a nail, or curl up under warm covers, we protect the child in us. It's natural to want to feel safe and protected, comforted and soothed.

So it's perfectly logical that a child is going to do the same thing. You may see:

- toddlers who have been walking confidently begin to crawl again
- bedwetting, sometimes into the teen years
- thumb sucking, lip chewing, nail biting, and other self-touching
- baby talk
- the need for a nightlight left on or a door left open
- clinging and whining
- climbing into a parent's bed
- cuddling with a favorite stuffed toy that had been packed away

- renewed interest in games and activities given up years ago
- continued need for reassurance and normal routine.

And there are more. Often this is a time when laps are needed more than usual and it's a great opportunity to read to young children, particularly books about death, which can trigger questions. Let them know that you, too, need things that comfort you and give you safety. Usually, regressive behavior doesn't last very long, but if you become concerned, talk to your child. Tell her it's okay to do this now and then, that you understand. Let her know, too, that you are confident that very shortly she'll be her old self again. Giving your child some undivided time each day, even if you yourself want to curl up and suck your thumb, helps. One mother took advantage of both and snuggled up in bed with her son. They talked and talked and both sucked their thumbs. It only took three times before both felt a lot better and went on to other things.

25

^^^

GRIEF AND PLAY

Tony Sims, director of Accord, an aftercare service working with funeral directors and grieving families, describes children who are grieving. "Children aren't linear," Tony says. "They're random access." Children will grieve, then play, grieve, then play. In the same video where Tony makes his random access observation (*Children Grieve, Too*), Judy Rubertino describes her children after her son Vinnie, age four, was killed by a drunk driver.

"I couldn't understand it," she says. "I was devastated and crying all the time, but my youngest daughter would cry for five minutes, then she'd go play, and in another five minutes my teenager would be on the telephone." Judy came to see this as the normal, natural childhood grief pattern. She talked to her parents and told them to expect it. The grandparents were expecting the children to grieve for longer stretches of time. Judy talked to teachers. The teachers were expecting the children to be involved in longer stretches of play.

There are two aspects to the grieving child and play:

1. the play/grieve/play cycle
2. the play of grief

Remember my cousin Ron, who was shivering under the covers as his mother was dying? Later that evening I lay in my bed and heard my father chasing him around the house. Both were laughing and playing. My little cousin, totally overwhelmed one minute, was hooting and squealing the next in a riotous game with a loving uncle.

To grieve, then play, then grow: This is the way of children. We could learn a lot from them.

26

SCHOOL WORK

A woman in our bereavement support group told about going back to work two weeks after her husband died. "I became an expert in computer games," she said. "That's all I could do."

Just as we adults become disoriented and numbed after a death, just as our work falls off and we stop our full functioning, so also do children. When your child is grieving, you can expect:

- lack of concentration
- a drop in grades or, in some cases, a sudden spurt in over-achieving
- either a more intense relationship with friends or increased isolation

It's important to advocate for children at this time. Teachers need to be notified that there has been a death in the family. Judy Rubertino, whom we mentioned earlier, went to school, talked to her children's teachers, and told them their little brother had been killed. "Don't come down hard on them if they start to cry in class," she told them. "Tell them it's okay to take a few minutes in the bathroom or the hallway. We've taught them some coping skills and they'll be all right in just a little while."

Judy didn't stop there. She visited the principal and the school counselor, both of whom were helpful, supportive, and eager to work with her to help her children.

There will be times at school when the grieving child is put on the spot, possibly embarrassed and at a loss for words. Children need time and some education in knowing how to ask for help. It doesn't come naturally for anyone at any age.

> "The first time
> I remember crying
> after my dad's death
> happened the next year at school.
> Someone in class asked why I didn't have a dad.
> Other kids were there, too, and they asked me where he
>   was.
> I told them he was dead.
> I could feel a lump swelling up in my throat,
> and it was hard to talk.
> Someone asked, "What is dead?"
> And I cried in front of them.
> I cried there at school.
> Another time,
> we made presents for our parents.
> All the kids in my class made one for their dads,
> I didn't have a dad to make one for.
> I cried right there at school, again.
> Once, the next spring,
> I heard my big brother talking to my mom after supper.
> He was really sad.
> He told her the guys at school had been talking
> about doing field work,
> and getting the soil ready to plant the spring seeds.
> They would be working with their dads.
> My brother was really feeling lonesome for our dad.
> I heard him crying that night."
> By Dorothy Ferguson, from *Saturday Night Mulberries*.

There are many resources within a school. You can ask for support, help, and advice from school counselors and psychologists, social workers, and others. Oftentimes the school counselor is one of the best listeners around and, if alerted to a child's grief, can be a real asset.

Some teachers have, with great sensitivity, talked with the grieving child and asked how that child wanted her classmates to know about what has happened. There have been sharing sessions on grief where entire classrooms talked about loved ones who had died, their ideas of death, and how to really be a friend when something sad occurs.

When grades drop, help is available through teachers and counselors, tutors and friends. Just recognizing that this is normal and will pass can give the child the confidence to improve concentration. When grades suddenly rise, it may be because the child is diving into schoolwork to escape the grief. This, too, will pass. The danger comes when grades are shaky or there is radical change for more than a semester or so. Then is the time for some counseling and some activities to work through grief.

Part Ten

GROWING UP FAST

27

BIG MAN, BIG WOMAN

Many of us have seen it and some of us have acted it out, but it was Alan Wolfelt, a leader in bereavement education who labeled it "Big Man" or "Big Woman" syndrome. This is the opposite of regression and often happens when a child tries to grow up quickly to take the place of the person who died, usually a parent.

Jordan, the beautiful young woman who married our grandson, Alex, is a good example. Her father died just before she was thirteen. By the time she was sixteen, she was working two jobs, buying the groceries, giving her family $175 a week, and making most of the major decisions. Today, Jordan is nobody's fool. She's one capable, dynamic, independent woman and we're lucky to have her in our family. However, she was basically robbed of a childhood, and even though she did what she did willingly, there's a tone of sadness in her voice when she talks about that time. She's done hard work to get over the anger and bitterness that almost anyone would encounter in a like situation. She feels it was her father's influence that gave her such a strong sense of responsibility.

I remember my cousin Ron standing at his mother's casket with his arm around his dad. We all grow up when someone dies, but as Marion Cohen wrote in *She Was Born: She Died*

"It matures you, they say,
It helps you grow up, they tell me,
So wasn't I mature enough before?"

If you see your child acting suddenly mature and overly grown up, it may be time to look at your own behavior and needs. It may be a way of protecting herself for a short time during her grief, to know things can still be brought under control. But if you are depending on your child to see you through your own grief and take over duties of a dead spouse, it may be time to have a talk with a bereavement counselor and to let your child know it is very important for her to be a kid right now. You may want to tell her you need her hugs and support and love and sometimes her help, but that she doesn't have to be a big woman. She doesn't have to be in charge. That's your job, even though you are grieving. Let her know you appreciate her hard work and that you know you can count on her when you do ask for help. We don't tend to have a second chance at a real childhood and we all deserve one.

Although I've used the word *she* in the above illustration, I truly believe that it is still the little boys in our culture who get the strongest and the most frequent Big Man messages. Men die earlier and in more accidents than do women and we still hear people tell even very small boys, "You're the man of the house now." No child deserves that burden.

28

~~~~~~

TEEN EXPECTATIONS

Up to this point, the conversations we've had about children and grief have centered mostly on younger children. Adolescents warrant a closer look.

Until after World War II, there virtually was no teenage period in our lives. To be a teenager is a new development. No wonder we sometimes don't have a clue as to what is going on. We're all amateurs even though we've lived through it ourselves and raised children through the teenage years. My grandmother was married at age sixteen; so was my mother. Born in 1938, I was the first generation in my family to have this "teenage" period. No wonder my parents mumbled to themselves a lot when I was fifteen.

The single most beautiful book written about children and grief is Alan Wolfelt's *Healing the Bereaved Child,* in which he describes the tender concept of *grief gardening* in caring for grieving children. Alan sees adolescence as a June garden, lush and full of life but still needing care and help from the gardener. The description of adolescent rage Alan gives helps explain the immense anger often expressed by teens: "The adolescent's heightened emotions often take the form of rage after a sudden death. Anger is a way for the teen to say, 'I protest this death' and to vent her feelings of helplessness."

Our son-in-law, Ben, was sixteen when his nineteen-year-old brother, Tim, was murdered. Janet, our daughter, was Tim's friend and met Ben when he came to help his parents collect his brother's belongings. Ben, who has worked with us at Centering Corporation for years now, has become a consultant on teen grief and regularly is called in to talk to school groups about death and grief.

Ben has good advice for parents and caregivers about what to expect and what not to expect from grieving teens: "Treat the teen as a young adult, an individual. Give him space. Allow him to grieve without minimizing or belittling his feelings. Let him know you will listen to him if he wants to talk to you.

"Teens may feel uncomfortable talking in front of family because they're afraid of bringing up unwanted feelings in both themselves and the listener. Don't worry about repressing or controlling those feelings. Cry together when you can.

"There may be some outward expressions of grief. I really put up a wall around my feelings. I tried to make myself invisible but that wasn't the effect it had. I dressed differently, wore black all the time, wore dark glasses, delved into art and music—both listening to it and writing and playing it. It was offensive to my parents. The basic thing is that anyone—teen or not—who goes through something like that is going to change, no matter what. Expectations should not be placed on any of us that we're going to be just like we were. We'll never be quite the same again."

Jacque Bell, a child life specialist who has worked with and written about grieving teens, adds additional good advice: "I really enjoy working with grieving teens. One thing parents and caregivers can expect is a huge brick wall. Adolescents think if they take the wall down they may not get it back up and it's tough enough dealing with the emotions that are on their side of the wall, not to mention the other side. Teens tend to seek information and support from very specialized others, such as a favorite school teacher, a pastor, or a loving uncle. Let them have license to do that and, in fact, encourage them to do that. Tell your teen, "If you're not able to share with me, you need to share with someone. My feelings won't be hurt if you talk to someone else, and I know that if you don't talk to someone, we can expect some behaviors that aren't healthy such as closing up, having lots more anger, and maybe not eating right and feeling depressed and even more sad." Treating your teen with real respect and sharing your own feelings, even it if appears your child isn't listening, can be valuable to you both."

Part Eleven

SPECIAL RELATIONSHIPS

29

RELATIONSHIPS TO THE DECEASED

I sometimes think of grief as being like the arrival of the Mother Ship in the movie classic *Close Encounters of the Third Kind*. In the movie the great ship descends, hovers, and begins to communicate through musical tones. One tone is so powerful the windows of the humans' control tower shatter. Grief is like that. There are different tones . . . a tone for the death of a child, a tone for a parent's death, another little tone when a beloved pet dies. They all combine to create the symphony of grief.

How children, and adults as well, grieve depends on the "tone" or the intensity of the relationship to the person who died. A child whose grandfather helped raise him, and was a best buddy with quarters for candy machines, will feel a great deal more sorrow and sadness than the little boy described by one of the masters of grief education, Rabbi Earl Grollman. A four-year-old boy was brought to Earl for counseling because his parents felt he was not grieving the death of his grandfather. When Rabbi Grollman said to the child, "It must be sad, having your grandfather die," the little boy looked at him and very honestly said, "I don't know. I only met him twice and both times he had bad breath."

It's important for us to be aware of the significance of the child's relationship to the loved person. We need to be sure we don't belittle the attachment by saying things such as

"You hardly knew him," and to avoid the terrible "shouldn'ts," such as "You shouldn't be sad. He was only a dog." Let the child tell you about the relationship, how it was important, and what it meant to that child. Let's face it, some folks we just won't miss all that much. Others will live in our hearts forever.

30

HELPFUL ACTIVITIES

A relationship doesn't die along with the body of the person. The relationship simply changes. There are several things we as well as children can do to make that relationship change a healthy one.

Sharon's son was killed in a fiery automobile crash. Her teenage daughter seemed to be doing as well as could be expected, then Sharon began to feel her grief was more severe than normal, more long-lasting, and more intense. She sat with her daughter and asked, "What is the worst part of all this?" Her daughter was quick to reply. "Oh! The picture!"

"What picture?" Sharon asked.

"The one in my head of Chris in the car. Every time I think of him, all I can see is the car burning up and his body burning up inside of it."

Sharon could relate to that. The accident had been terrible. To make matters worse, the local newspaper had carried a front-page picture of the wreckage, her son's running shoe laying forlornly on its side next to the car.

A few days later, Sharon called her daughter to her. "I have an idea that may help us both," she said. "The next time you see Chris burning in the car, keep that picture in your head for a second. Then take another picture. Remember a happy time, a happy place, what was happening. Remember the smells and the laughter and exactly what your brother looked like, what he said, and what he was doing. Take a mental picture of that. Then, just like on your computer, make a file in another part of your head. Take at least five 'happy pictures' and put them in the Happy Memories File Folder—or whatever you want to label it. The next time you see Chris burning in the car, open your file folder and put one of the happy pictures over the sad one. Do that until you've brought out all the happy pictures."

The first "picture" Sharon's daughter took was of her brother coming out of the bathroom after his shower, a towel wrapped around his waist and another one around his head because being in a family with four sisters, he didn't know you didn't have to wrap your hair in a towel if it was really short. The coping technique worked. Gradually there were more happy memories than frightening and sad ones.

Grief often needs a physical outlet, especially with children.

Modeling or *sculpting* is one helpful coping activity that can assuage anger and restlessness as well as provide a creative outlet. Plain old modeling clay works just fine and can be reused over and over again. As the child forms the clay, energy flows into it. Helen Fitzgerald tells of a girl whose friend had been murdered. She modeled a man holding a knife and standing over the dead child. After the little girl talked about how angry she was, she pounded the figure with her fist until it was nothing but a lump of clay. If you can also model something and share what it is and what feeling it represents, you can create interesting and meaningful conversations and sharing with your child as well as some pretty fantastic forms, shapes, and figures.

Journaling is perhaps one of the most respected and constructive forms of coping for all ages. More and more schools are starting children out in early grades with their own journals, and as we have said before, in some ways it's a cheap psychiatrist. Any child who can write or print can journal. You can give the child a guided journal, such as those listed in the back of this book, or you can give him a ringed notebook and blank paper or even a tablet or spiral-bound school notebook . . . anything with blank surfaces.

Colored pens, ballpoint pens, pencils, crayons, anything that helps with art adds to the experience. The journal needs to be personal and private unless the child *wants* to share it. Some families have made personal journals and private journals: one to be shared, one for the writer's eyes only. Journals can contain pictures, drawings, song lyrics, poems, and pages and pages of feelings. Letters to the dead person and letters of response can also be part of the process.

Letters both to the dead person and in response are part of coping. The most dramatic healing I have witnessed from letter writing occurred in my own family. Nineteen years before I was born, my parent's three-year-old daughter, Roena, died of pneumonia. My mother was so devastated she decided never to have more children. Nearly 20 years later, when she learned I was on the way, she decided that at least she wouldn't have to have another little girl. It took her five days after I was born to be convinced that "Donald" was probably not a name I would be comfortable with as I grew older.

For as long as I can remember, my mother was sick. There were migraine headaches and surgeries and trip after trip to doctor after doctor. Remember, in those days there were no books on grief. There were no support groups. Also, for as long as I can remember, my mother kept a safe distance from me through bickering, criticism, and avoidance. When she was in her mid-seventies, she called, worried that she would have to have yet another surgery. Suddenly she said, "You know, ever since Roena died, I just haven't felt good." I was amazed. I had training now in death and grief, yet I had been too close to the situation all these years to see it for what it was—complicated mourning. I became firm with her. "Here's what I want you to do," I told her. "You sit down tonight and write a letter to Roena and you tell her everything you want to tell her. Then you write a letter back to you from her and you listen to what she has to say." Mother sighed. "Well," she said, "I'll try."

I didn't hear from her for three days, then the call came. Her voice was tired. "I just want to thank the Good Lord and you," she said. (I say it's second billing but not bad company.) She continued. "I feel as if a burden of 50-some years has been lifted from me and I don't think it will come back." It didn't. Mother lost weight, became remarkably healthy and active, and fell in love some 20 years after my father had died.

When I cleaned out Mother's house after her death, I looked for the Roena letters. I found them in an old Bible that was held together by a lady's old-fashioned garter. There was a bright yellow stationery envelope, the kind you use for loving and important correspondence. Inside were two sheets of paper. I pulled them out, filled with anticipation. The first said,

> "Dear Roena,
> I'm going to let you go. I know you're with your Daddy. I know you're happy now. I will always love you.
> Mommy"

The second sheet said,

> "Dear Mommy,
> I'm very happy here with Daddy. I love you too and I don't want you to cry anymore.
> Love, Roena"

That's all it took! I would have sat at my computer and typed five pages, all right-justified and in a small font. The important thing is to physically (through writing) make a contact (emotional) with that part of yourself that connects to the person who died. People we love always live in our hearts. They may die, but we don't lose them.

Everything that helps you and your child remember happy times and find a new normal is a coping technique. My mother and aunts were large ladies and ordered their shoes and clothes, including old-fashioned girdles, from a company known as National Belles Hess. It was a very important part of their lives and a staple for ladies in the 1930s and '40s. When Marv and I did a workshop in the city where the Belles Hess factory had been, I found a brochure announcing that it had been turned into a museum. I walked happily through the museum, imagining that my two aunts and mother were with me, enjoying every bit of it, looking through the old catalogs so carefully preserved. I could imagine them pointing and laughing and having a wonderful time. It was refreshing and loving and fun. They are always with us. Even now, when I enter a shop that displays beautiful, classy porcelain chickens, I say, "Look at that one, Mom!" She had what she called a "Great Chicken Collection." Recently my daughter saw a huge ceramic rooster in a window and remarked how much Grandma would have loved that. Good memories.

We do not have a choice of whether or not we grieve; we grieve. We do have a choice of *how* we grieve and a choice of finding new, creative ways to cope.

Part Twelve

RELIGION AND GRIEF

31

SHARING YOUR FAITH

D iAngelo was four when his brother, Rochelle, died of sudden infant death syndrome. "Rocky" had been dead for only a few weeks when Halloween came around. DiAngelo went to his mother and with a very serious face asked, "Do we think Rocky is an angel?" Mom thought for a minute then said, "Yes, I guess you could say that," at which time DiAngelo went to their sliding glass door, opened it, went out onto their deck, and looking up at the sky yelled, "Hey Rocky! Come down for Halloween! You can wear your angel suit!"

Children take things very literally. They are concrete thinkers. This may mean that no matter how hard you try to explain your religious beliefs, you're more than likely going to miss something. Joey was five when his grandmother died. His parents had done a good job with their little boy. They used the real words such as "dead" and "died." Joey picked out the necklace Gram would wear in the casket. He touched her, drew a picture to put in with her, and was in the front row with the rest of his family during the service. Almost immediately after the funeral he developed an unusual fear of the telephone.

When the phone rang, Joey either cried, stopped dead in his tracks and became pale, or went running for his bedroom where his father would find him hiding in his closet. After the third time this happened, Joey's parents sat down with him and asked him what was going on. Without a minute's hesitation, the little five year old said, "It may be God and we shouldn't answer it!"

During the funeral the minister had used a very common phrase. God had called Grandma home. Joey wasn't taking any calls.

It's important to share your faith with you child. In Joey's case, even though his folks had encouraged him to ask questions about anything that puzzled or bothered him, Joey thought it was very clear what to ask and what to avoid. The best advice here is to keep an eye open and an ear ready to listen.

It can be very confusing for a child to see his brother in a casket and at the same time be told he's in heaven. It's troubling for a child to be told his father's death is part of God's plan when Daddy was gunned down in a random killing. And to hear that God wanted her mother because she was so good is a written invitation for her daughter to stop being good, no matter what.

Rabbi Earl Grollman, who through his writing and speaking helped change the way the world treats grieving children, says it very well in his book *Talking About Death—A Dialogue Between Parent and Child*. In his section called "Explaining About an Afterlife," Rabbi Grollman starts out with an example of what *not* to say. " '*We can't be selfish,*' the father said, seeking to ease his son's pain. '*God was lonely and wanted Mommy in heaven.*' " Earl goes on: "The concept of heaven is difficult for a child to grasp. '*But Daddy, if Mommy is going to heaven, then why are they putting her in the ground?*' Some children peer from an airplane window seeking the loved one. Others hope rain coming down from heaven will bring the loved one back to earth.

"You may feel your own beliefs are too stark for a youngster—that it would be more comforting to express a religious conviction that you do not personally hold. So you spin out a tale of heavenly happiness while hopeless finality fills your own heart. Children have built-in radar and quickly detect your inconsistency and deception. Share honest religious convictions, but be prepared for further questions concerning simplistic theological terms. Religious convictions can bring comfort and understanding to children if they are carefully explained."

It's very tempting to paint a rosy picture, a perfect place called heaven. I clearly remember my mother and aunts talking about literal concepts, much like what children hold. "There will be pearly gates," my mother would say. "And the streets are all paved with gold," my Aunt Ada would add. Good old Aunt Bess would put in the really practical word, "And there isn't any pain and people are happy all the time." They would sigh in unison. "And we'll see all our folks," Mother would say, pulling out her handkerchief. That was the cue. They would talk about Grandma and Uncle Norval, who died when he was thirty, and the babies and then they'd look at me, staring in a minor state of panic, and Aunt Ada would say, "Every girl needs a good cry now and then." The danger is that a too-perfect picture can lead a child to want to go there, to a place where the hurt is gone and where the loved one isn't dead anymore. It's rare, but children have tried to kill themselves or to will themselves dead to get to that perfect place and have a reunion with the person who just died.

The opposite, of course, is true when God becomes the villain, the bad guy. It's so easy to say, "God took him." We don't believe God calls people to heaven like some celestial social director because they're wanted there more than here. William Sloan Coffin, a famous theologian, told how he believed that when the waters of the river closed over the top of his son's car, God's heart was the first to break. God doesn't pull triggers, dump cars off bridges, or push little children in front of trains. God grieves with us.

When a loved one dies, you have a tremendous opportunity to share your religious beliefs and faith with your child. Getting that faith into simple, concrete terms can be a real challenge to you. Remember the little boy who wanted to know what God was driving? His mother told him his brother would die, *then* God would come get his soul. She avoided making God into a people snatcher.

One theologian said, "The Bible doesn't promise quick fixes. It promises support and love, support and love, support and love." In offering your own support and love to your child you can:

- share what you believe about death and God
- take your child for a visit with your minister, priest, or rabbi. If you don't have a clergy person, call your local hospital or hospice and ask for the number of a chaplain who knows something about grief and can talk to children.
- give your child lots of permission to ask questions.

32

YOUR CHILD AND YOUR PLACE OF WORSHIP

Churches are really beginning to work with grief and grievers. The Stephen Ministries School Class provides excellent listeners through lay people who care deeply. Many churches have bereavement support programs. We're getting there.

However, no matter how loving and caring your church or synagogue is, you're still likely to run into what Dr. Susan Holtkamp, in her book *Grieving With Hope*, calls "Demented Spiritual Cheerleaders." These are people who truly want to make things better but are awkward in their approach. Theirs is the "if you have faith you won't grieve" attitude. Of course you grieve! No matter how deep your faith, you miss your spouse, your child, your parent. To *not* grieve is to show a lack of faith—faith that your tears are a gift from God and meant to be used.

If your child is part of a youth or children's group, talk with the leader. Just as you advocate for your child in the school system, you advocate for your child in the church system.

One grandmother was on her church's prayer chain. Her family loyally prayed with her every day. One day her ten-year-old granddaughter told her, "Mom says you will get well,

Nana. She says we are praying for you to be cured every day and God always answers prayers." Nana was stunned. The next time her family gathered to pray she looked them all straight in the eye, one by one, and said, "Let's all get this straight. You are praying for the wrong thing here! Pray I may be *healed*, not cured. Just remember that perhaps the most healing thing for me now is to die. *That* may be the way God answers this prayer."

Reverend Richard Gilbert, who does numerous workshops on grief for clergy, says, "Recognizing grief means advocating for children, affirming their value, needs, and rights, as children of God who experience loss and need to grieve. It means we have to take the risk and deal with dying and what death means to us in our own lives. We need to affirm death as *part of life*, not the enemy of it. We need to be people who are willing to see a different sense of life that comes to us, even in death."

One of our friends, whose daughter completed suicide, said to our Sunday School group, "You are the people who got us through this. If it were not for your love, we could never have made it." Debbie's ashes are buried beside a rose bush near the front of the church. That is the kind of love and care people of faith can radiate. Our task is to be sure it shines on our children as well.

Part Thirteen

THEORIES AND THEMES

There may well come a time when you're experiencing your finest moment in teaching a child about death and grief and from behind you a voice says, "So how come you know so much about all this?" We all need a basic background of ideas from people who have worked with and studied children and grief and how all of us of all ages react and cope when we're faced with death. Here we present the very basic ones.

33

~~~~~~

FOUR COMMON THEMES

T hrough all the theories, ideas, and insights run four common elements of how grief affects all of us, children as well as adults. It affects us physically, mentally, emotionally, and spiritually.

Physically

Our body grieves. The most obvious sign of physical grief comes through tears. Children, especially younger ones who are not yet "contaminated" with social restrictions, show their grief openly with vivid body language. They cry. They pout. They hit and kick and let grief run through their little bodies like a toy train on a fast track. Tell a child he can't have feelings and you might want to protect your shins.

Elizabeth Kingsley, Ph.D., a psychologist in Kansas City, Missouri, says the impact of the news and realization of grief hits us right in our primitive brain stem area. It moves in like a tornado and arouses all our fight or flight responses. We're highly aware of the feelings, smells, and sounds. We are ready to run, to fight, and at the same time, we're immobilized.

Our job as grievers is to move all those sensory, feeling experiences into the verbal area of our brains. The brain stem is that part that connects the back of our heads to our necks. The verbal part is in the front of our brain. Once we start moving all the feelings and sensations into words, we can begin to talk about our experience. We can talk and talk and talk about it. We can write about it, sing it out, dance, and draw our feelings. Unless we can do so, and often even when we do, the brain stem overflows with emotions. The intense feelings have to move out to make room for future stimuli, so they spread into our bodies.

Moving the story and impact from our brain stems to our verbal area lets us *frame* our story. In framing, we tell the same story over and over again. Each time we tell it, the story becomes clearer to us, the paragraphs gradually take shape, the commas go where they should. The story goes from eighteen pages in the telling to three. Finally, the story is concise, easier to tell, and makes sense. It's understandable. We've framed our story. Now we can hang it on the wall. We can take it down when we want to and look at it and change it, but we don't have to carry it around with us all the time. A fourteen-year-old girl once said to us, "My mom carries a picture of my dead brother with her all the time." We smiled knowingly and wisely said, "Well, you know we really encourage that." The girl smiled. "A framed eight by ten?" she asked. Once the story is framed, it weighs less, is easier to handle, and is more readily shared. It's never forgotten, it's just more concise. Remember, anything can be borne if a story can be told. Framing is how we get our story into our verbal center and makes it tellable.

Our entire immune system is affected by grief and the roller coaster of feelings that go with it. We know for a fact that after someone dies, children are far more likely to catch a cold. Most have stomach aches. We adults ache, too. As one father whose child died said, "My arms ached." Children as well as adults have headaches as well as heartaches. Children wet the bed; we get up in the middle of the night and go to the bathroom. Children lose their appetites; nothing tastes good to us. Children sit and stare and feel numb. So do we. The increase in doctor visits skyrockets after a death in the family. Often many family members complain of the same symptoms their loved one experienced.

Other symptoms include sighing because we aren't breathing normally. We tend to hold our breath when we grieve. We also don't drink as much water and we're crying much more. We get dehydrated easily. We tell grieving individuals to put a pitcher on the cupboard with eight glasses of water in it and know they will drink that during the day. Luckily, children tend to grieve, play, and grieve. During play their bodies regain strength and health. It's a good idea to keep close track of illnesses and get children and yourself to a doctor whenever you become concerned.

Linda Goldman, in her excellent book *Life and Loss*, lists the physical symptoms many grieving children experience:

headaches	pounding heart	empty feeling in body
fatigue	hot or cold flashes	tightness in chest
shortness of breath	heaviness of body	muscle weakness
dry mouth	sensitive skin	tightness in throat
dizziness	increased illness	stomach aches

Mentally

We are a people who need answers. "Why?" often becomes the favorite word of two and three year olds. We use the same word as adults as we try to make sense of death, and some deaths seem totally senseless. It's the mental part of grief that gives children the multitude of questions that flood parents and caregivers. It's the mental part of grief that forces us as adults to go over and over and over the death, the causes, the *if only* agonies. *If only* I had gotten her to the doctor sooner, *if only* I had stopped for five minutes before getting into the car—mental questions that tie into our emotions.

Children will ask questions, get the answers they need, and go out to play. As they grow, they ask different questions. A five year old is satisfied that Grandma's heart stopped. A twelve year old wants to know what part of the heart caused the death and what the illness was called.

Our task as adults is to make all the mental images, all the questions, and all the knowledge we have about the death and about grief compatible with what we feel in our hearts. Our heads and hearts need to be in line. Often we *know* something mentally, but our heart doesn't believe it.

Carolyn *knew* mentally that she could not have stopped Wayne from climbing onto the chair to reach the paint can on the shelf over the stairs. She *knew* mentally that she could not have grabbed him before he fell headlong to his death at the foot of the stairs. She *knew*. But she didn't believe it. She didn't get the knowing from her head to her gut or her heart until she sat down and wrote a letter to Wayne apologizing and saying she should have been able to do something. Then she wrote the letter back from him, and in it she recorded his laughter at her predicament. "You think you could have convinced me not to climb up there?" she wrote from the Wayne within her. "And who do you think you are to want to grab that damn chair: Wonder Woman?"

In addition to all the questions and agony we think about mentally when we're grieving, two other things happen:

1. Our minds go numb. There is a joke about aging that goes: "At my age I'm thinking a lot about the hereafter. I go into room after room, stand there and say, 'Now what am I here after?' " Kay called me one day and said, "The tapes you loaned me were victims of my grief." She had taken a set of tapes with her to her car, put them on the roof, opened the car, gotten in, and driven off, leaving the tapes flying behind her into the street. Parents have stood in the grocery store staring for ten full minutes trying to decide between the peas and the beans. We can't think. Our minds are blank. Our mental function simply slows way down and sometimes stops altogether. This is a protective mechanism and tells us to take care of ourselves until we're over the shock.

2. We're stimulated mentally. We search for answers. We read everything we can about grief and death. We demand the autopsy report and we talk to others who have been in the same situation. A doctor told us once there were two kinds of families who spoke to her after someone died. Family A wanted to know everything about everything. They wanted answers, details, and technical information. Family B was just the opposite and much like my mother, who once said, "If I ever have cancer, don't anybody tell me! I don't want to know." My father and most of her family had died of the disease. Unfortunately, so did she, and fortunately, she did know. She faced it, made decisions, and died a very dignified death. Mother's thought patterns had changed after she faced her fears and came to terms with her terminal illness. Like the roller coaster of emotions that come with grief, adults and children alike have thought patterns

that come and go, and, as one twelve year old explained, "are like tornadoes in the brain."

Linda Goldman's very precise list of thought patterns found in grieving children include:

inability to concentrate	preoccupation
difficulty making a decision	confusion
self-destructive thoughts	disbelief
low self-image	

Emotionally

We've talked a lot about the emotional aspects of grief. Children cry, as do we adults. The emotions of grief are like a roller coaster with dramatic ups and downs. Children need to know their feelings will level out eventually; that every day won't be a bad day.

It can be difficult for us adults to allow children their emotions. We want to make them feel better, to fix it, to make things right, and we can't do that after a death. Children need to feel the sorrow, know the anger, and walk through the fear and anxiety that comes with new experiences. Again, Linda Goldman makes it easy for us in her *Life and Loss* list of feelings:

anger	depression	fear	intense feelings
guilt	hysteria	loneliness	feeling unreal
sadness	relief	anxiety	
mood swings	helplessness	rage	

Without our emotions we are nothing. We are nonfeelers and when we don't feel, we don't live. If we love, we will grieve. As Darcie Sims says, "The truly bereaved are those who never love."

It's our emotions combined with our mental activity that guide our behaviors. Grieving adults say more than once, "I can't believe I did that!" We say of others, "She's just not herself since he died." Our actions change as well as our ways of thinking. This combination of feelings and thinking reflect the behaviors of grieving children. Linda Goldman lists these, too:

sleeplessness	sighing	verbal attacks
loss of appetite	listlessness	fighting
poor grades	absent-mindedness	extreme quietness
crying	clinging	bed-wetting
nightmares	overactivity	excessive touching
dreams of deceased	social withdrawal	excessive hugging

Remember, all these feelings, physical symptoms, and behaviors are reflections of normal grief in children, and usually adults as well.

Spiritually

Spirituality is different from religion. Religion is the organized expression of faith, shared in a community of believers. Spirituality is that part of ourselves that connects in some way with a being of higher power, a faith system, and deeply held personal beliefs.

Children's spirituality often reflects that of their parents, but can also be seen in their very tender trust and faith. Their questions about God and death and what happens after we die reflect their spiritual questions. Because of their trust and because at an early age children take things literally, it's our job to teach them of a loving God who cares for them and us, who cries with us when we grieve. It's important to make sure children don't see God as a people snatcher or the villain who pulled the trigger or pushed the car off the road.

For those families with religious and spiritual foundations, allowing and encouraging the child to join in prayers and rituals that commemorate the dead person can be vitally important. Feelings can be offered up to God and be affirmed. For many, this offers a sense of security and meaning in life. However, it is also perfectly all right for children to express anger at God when someone dies. At that time it's appropriate to let the child know that God can listen to anything he says and will offer only unconditional love in return. Basically, the message to give children is that God understands and loves them.

34

MAJOR THEORIES

During the last 20 years, more and more attention has been directed toward the grieving child. Through it all, several major ideas have been presented and have dove-tailed beautifully to give us a good, solid picture of what to expect from and how to support, educate, and love grieving children. There are many theories, and here I've chosen four people whose theories are laid out clearly: Elisabeth Kubler-Ross, Sandra Fox, Alan Wolfelt, and Donna O'Toole. Others appear throughout this book, ready and willing to help us care for our children.

Elisabeth Kubler-Ross

Dr. Ross is the Grand Dame of death and dying. Her book *On Death and Dying* was first published in 1969. She was the first to visit with dying patients and because of it she was called "The Vulture." She faced death down and looked it over from stem to stern. She lifted up the black pall that covered it and found out what was underneath. We owe her a lot.

Just recently someone said to me, "I learned that the *stages* Kubler-Ross listed applied to the dying, not the grieving."

"Same thing," I replied. "When I am dying, I am grieving. When I am grieving, a part of me is dying."

Kubler-Ross named the feelings we have when we are dying and grieving. When you name something you have control over it, you have power, you have the means by which to tackle it head on and cope. Unfortunately, the label "stages" led some people to believe grief was linear—that it came in step one, step two, and so on. Actually, those stages come all mixed up. They come in waves. What is important here is the definition of the feelings. Kubler-Ross listed:

Denial and Isolation

When we first learn of our diagnosis or the terminal diagnosis or death of a loved one, we're paralyzed, stunned, immobilized. Younger children don't experience this in the same way as adults. They are more likely to express doubt or surprise. Here we find ourselves saying, "not me!" or "can't be." Throughout our grief we will have short bursts of denial, from dreams of our loved one to imagining, just for a split-second, that we see our person. Denial helps us face reality more slowly, when we are ready. At the same time, we feel very alone—as if this has never happened to anyone else.

Anger

We've said a lot about this. It's the "why me!" question/exclamation. Usually "why?" is not so much a question asked as a statement to be heard.

Bargaining

"Okay, God. Make me well and I'll . . ." Fill in the blanks. "Look, Doc, you give me the right medicine and I'll . . ." We bargain with God, the staff, our family, our bodies. Our mind is busy finding ways to get well or get over grief. Children can easily get into magical thinking here, and we aren't far behind them.

Depression and Withdrawal

We can't lose anything or anybody without feeling sad. There are times when we have to hit bottom before we can get up again.

Acceptance

For the dying person, this is the time when goodbyes are said and restful curiosity begins. For the griever, it's as a friend said, "My daughter died 16 years ago and finally I can say, 'It's okay that you died.' "

It is appropriate to recognize these ideas from Elisabeth Kubler-Ross, especially when it comes to children. Over and over she emphasized that they were not "stages—as in one, two, three"—but processes. Children, who are not linear but random access, demonstrate well how each feeling can come and go at any time.

Sandra Fox

Another early pioneer in children's grief was Sandra Fox, who died a few years ago. She had worked with many grieving children and listed their grief work simply and clearly as "Tasks of Grieving: Understanding, Grieving— Feeling the Feelings, Commemorating, and Moving On."

Understanding occurs when the child knows the person is dead and not coming back. They have a basic understanding of what death is and that it is permanent.

Grieving—Feeling the feelings happens when the child can feel the sorrow and do the mourning that is the outward expression of grief.

Commemorating means keeping the memories alive. Children have suggested that a dead brother's Christmas stocking be hung and filled with toys to be given to a children's charity, birthday cakes have been baked and decorated by children whose mother died and served proudly on her birthday.

Moving on is the time when we engage in life again, living fully while still remembering the person. Often older children seek permission from family members and others to move on.

Alan Wolfelt

One of the current leaders in childhood bereavement, Alan Wolfelt, lists dimensions of childhood grief in his book, *Healing the Bereaved Child.* These move into a more detailed framework which is clearly and sensibly described and easy to understand.

Reconciliation
Loss/Emptiness/Sadness
Relief
Guilt and Self-Blame
Fear
Acting-Out Behavior
Explosive Emotions
Disorganization and Panic
"Big Man" or "Big Woman" Syndrome
Regression
Physiological Changes
Lack of Feelings
Shock/Denial/Disbelief/Numbness

Again, as with the Kubler-Ross descriptions, these dimensions are not to be taken as one–two–three steps to be followed, but as descriptions to guide us.

Donna O'Toole

Another leader in death education is Donna O'Toole, whose *Growing Through Grief* is an outstanding curriculum for all types of teachers. Her equally outstanding theory of grief is one of grief/growth:

Loss
Initial Impact

Shock
Safeguarding (Self-Protecting)
Anguish and Despair
Healing–Restructuring
Resolving
Growth

We've drawn on many people who represent some of the best in the field of childhood grief. Hopefully, from these short examples you can derive some knowledge and background. If not, hopefully you'll have the questions to delve further into each author's work.

Part Fourteen

SOMEONE'S DYING

35

~~~~~~

PREPARING FOR A VISIT

Earlier in this book I told about being held by my daddy and watching men carry my grandfather's body out of his house. Even at that early age I can remember going every weekend to be with my dying grandfather and his caregiver, my grandmother. The only time I really saw him was when I playfully scampered up and bounced on his bed. He was very, very ill then, and immediately my mother grabbed me and pulled me off while Grandma scolded, "Joy Kay, don't do that!" But before they pulled me off the bed, I had a look deep into his eyes. They sparkled as if he and I shared a great and funny secret, and he smiled a huge smile at me. He was too ill to speak, but I knew that my bouncing on his bed was quite all right. I didn't know him. He was thin as a skeleton. I liked him.

I was a real wimp when my father died. I visited him in the hospital. I didn't know beans about grief or death and I was uncomfortable. It was not until after he died that I told him how much I loved him. I know more now. I know to do differently.

When you take a child to visit a dying relative, prepare her first.

• *Ask if she wants to go visit.*

Often if a child says "No," it's because she's afraid of what may happen, what feelings may occur, and what she'll see. Ask her to talk about not wanting to go and tell her you'll explain everything she'll see and be with her all the time.

- *Be honest and ready for the big question.*
This is the time to say it straight out. "Gram is very, very sick and in the hospital." If the child asks, "Is she going to die?" it's safe to say something like, "Probably. The doctors and nurses are doing everything they can to make her comfortable, and we just don't know how long Gram will live."

- *Describe what she will see.*
If the person is in a hospital, describe any equipment that may be present and attached to the patient. Ask if the hospital has a child-life department and, if so, make an appointment to have a child-life specialist visit with your child before you see the dying person. Stay and listen to the specialist with your child so you can answer questions that may arise. Often the child-life specialist will be willing to accompany you when the child first sees your loved one.

- *Talk about what people will be doing.*
If there is family present, gathered around the bed or in and out in shifts, talk about the possibility of some confusion, hushed voices, worried looks, and tears. Make sure the child knows all these feelings are okay and normal. And as always, make sure the child knows he did not cause the illness, that he can't "catch" death, and that you'll still be a family no matter what.

- *Take a small gift.*
Helen Fitzgerald recommends taking a gift as a natural way to invite the child to talk to the patient and also as a way to say goodbye. A gift brings a pleasant memory and the child knows she has done something special for someone loved, even if that person can't enjoy it for very long. After the death, the child can place the gift in the casket.

• *Keep the visit short.*

After you leave, find time to talk to the child about what she saw, what she felt, and her general impressions.

We have known children who helped care for dying relatives who were cared for in their homes. Children have read to grandparents and fathers, brought soup to the bedside, drawn pictures for the room, and been an active part of caregiving. One thing we've learned for sure: Never underestimate a child, ever.

36

~~~~~~

THE DYING CHILD

We've all heard it many times and said it ourselves, "It's not natural to bury a child. Grown children should bury their parents instead." After all these years of working with families whose children have died, I'm not sure that statement is true. Every spring, during my walks in our neighborhood of giant trees, the nests yield up baby birds whose tiny bodies lie on the sidewalks. Many times I have gently moved them under their trees and covered them with leaves. Tom Mangelsen, a famous wild-life photographer, is shown in a documentary grieving as he photographs a mother polar bear licking the face of her dying twin baby. Young things die.

Children who are dying are also grieving. Whenever we die, no matter what our age, we grieve the loss of our "self." We grieve the loss of others as well. When someone I know dies, I lose one person, but when *I* die, I lose everyone and everything.

A child's prolonged illness throws the family into a chaotic uproar. Not only are emotions raw—fear, anxiety, worry, sadness, depression, anger, and more—but there is also a dramatic change in routine that now must include clinic and hospital visits. Parents may be absent from siblings for long periods of time. Gifts and concerns surround the ill child while sisters and brothers are neglected. Money, even with good insurance, becomes a tremendous concern. Parents are frequently sleep-deprived and exhausted. It's a tough time, indeed. Dan Rothermel, in his book *Sweet Dreams Robyn*, says it well:

> *As the intern arranges*
> *the vials of orange-colored medicine*
> *gauze and bandages*
> *needles and plastic tubes*
> *still I have no second thoughts*
> *no shades of gray*
> *I am their willing accomplice*
> *she sobs*
> *and submits*
> *I hold her arm*
> *look in her eyes*
> *I don't watch the needle*
> *but I bring my mouth*
> *to her ear*
> *the doctor needs*
> *just a little more blood*
> *honey.*

Dying children with whom we have worked have several concerns:

• *Fear of abandonment*

In truth, all of us of all ages have this fear. Children, more dependent than most adults, have an even greater fear. Dying children need to be reassured that someone who loves them will be with them no matter what, no matter when. Frequently, nurses and other hospital staff become a second family and can provide excellent support in letting the child know he will never be alone.

• *Family survival*

Dr. Lynn Bennett Blackburn, who wrote *Timothy Duck* and *The Class in Room 44*, tells how her dying son, D.J., asked the same question each time a young friend from his cancer clinic died: "Will his family be okay?" Children feel responsible. They care deeply. They need to know that after they die their families will (1) survive and move ahead into a new and different but still happy life and (2) always remember them. None of us wants to be forgotten.

- *Personal responsibility*

There is good news and bad news as our society becomes more and more accepting of complimentary medicine, meditation, and mind–body connections. The good news is that there are many options to help us heal. The bad news is that when everything fails we feel guilty. The child who hears that if she takes her medicine she'll be well is going to feel some guilt even if she's never spit out or hid a single pill. When Julie told her mother she was dying because she had hidden her medicine for a whole day, Angie reassured her strongly that one day would not make such a big difference. "There are just some things we can't explain, Julie," her mother told her. "We all fought hard. We did everything we could to make you well. We will always love you and we'll always miss you more than we can say. What you must do, though, is realize that we all did our very best and you were a strong, strong little soldier in this war and we love you and we really respect you for that."

- *Fear of the unknown*

As an aging Catholic cardinal reportedly said, "Oh God, I do not fear death . . . it is the dying!" There's not a one of us that walks into the unknown without a tiny bit of doubt, a little bit of wonder, and a good supply of awe. Dying children share many of the same fears of adults. We have a fear of pain, of loss of control over body functions, of what comes after death, and even of changes in our looks.

Traci, age seventeen, held a party before her first bout of chemotherapy. At the party, with her best friends sitting in a circle around her, her sister cut off her hair and handed a lock of it to each girl in the circle. Then her sister finished the job by shaving Traci's head. Her friends gathered around, felt her bones, commented on how neat she looked. Their gifts of the evening were scarves and clever hats for her to wear when her hair fell out. Traci took some control over her changing appearance and gathered her own support group at the same time.

In the beautiful book, *On the Wings of a Butterfly*, by Marilyn Maple, Lisa is ill and before her death befriends Sonya, a caterpillar who talks with her about change, and together they prepare for their deaths and transformations:

" 'Mom, Dad,' Lisa said, 'what happens after you die?' There was a short silence. Lisa's dad reached for her hand. Her mom put an arm around her shoulders.

" 'Well, honey,' said her dad, 'different people believe different things. Grandpa always said that when he died, he was going to be with God in a beautiful place called heaven.'

" 'I think that when we die, we change,' said Mom. 'We won't feel pain anymore and we'll be beautiful and peaceful. What is for sure though, Lisa, is that we will always love you—and when someone loves you, you are never alone.'

" 'That's good,' said Lisa. 'I'll always love you, too.' "

Elisabeth Kubler-Ross has said that dying children become like wise old people. Maybe that's because we treat them differently, are more honest with them, and become more involved in explaining their illness and in talking about what may happen as well as in sharing our beliefs. Whatever the reason, dying children are wonderful teachers. Susan Abbott, in her book, *Lessons*, says:

"I have learned that I cannot rush through grief.
The process is slow, tedious, and all-consuming.
Each phase must be traversed,
each feeling must be experienced, each tear must be al-
lowed to fall.
There are no short-cuts, no escapes, and no respites.
At my weakest point, I know I must continue.
I must persevere.
Very simply, each day I try to try
and, for me, the trying is the winning."

Part Fifteen

THE BIG QUESTIONS

37

AIDS

More and more families are being touched by AIDS, acquired immune deficiency syndrome. Some years ago, at one of our workshops, we asked for parents who had experienced the death of a child to come forward and be part of a panel. One of the nurses attending was a small woman with soft brown hair and big blue eyes. When she began to talk, the room fell silent. Tears streamed down her cheeks and down ours, too. This is what she said: "My son died of AIDS. He was a beautiful young man and he was a delight to us. He called from his apartment in New York and told us he was HIV positive. Our family is close and really neat and he had no problem years before when it came time to tell us he was gay. He knew we'd understand and that we loved him. Period. His illness advanced more rapidly than we thought. Just last month we all gathered at his home along with his partner, Jon, and stayed with him until he died. During his last day alive, we burned candles, played soft, classical music, and took turns holding him. It was a beautiful death for a beautiful person."

It doesn't matter how people get AIDS, whether from a sexual encounter, from needles, or from blood. Only the truly cruel see this disease as a punishment. Only the partially blind ignore the pain it brings to the person suffering from it and from the families losing those they love. When I was a little girl, people were so stigmatized by *cancer* that folks refused to speak the word. They became ill with "C" instead. It was a death sentence. People were discriminated against and isolated, not a lot different than the AIDS stigma today.

When one person in a family has AIDS, the whole family suffers. Children, whether they know about AIDS or not, will pick up on the family stress and may withdraw or become angry and frightened . . . just like the rest of us. More stress is added because often the family keeps the AIDS a secret to avoid ostracism or harassment. Early on, children whose sibling or family member had AIDS were thrown out of their schools and virtually locked inside their homes. Today we know better, but the labels and unkindness still exist.

Children are afraid of abandonment, especially if a parent and perhaps even the child himself is HIV (human immunodeficiency virus) positive and may come down with AIDS. They need reassurance that there will be someone there to care for them no matter what happens. This is a painful time for a child and we can help.

When a loved one has AIDS, it gets us back to

1. finding out what the children already know
2. being honest
3. answering questions

If the child is HIV positive, it's even more important to be truthful and supportive. You're also likely to have a parent who is infected and is often unable to work or function if the illness has gone to full-blown AIDS. In addition to being so very ill, many parents are afraid of becoming social outcasts and are often afraid of being attacked or experiencing violence. It's more than any family deserves. There are additional issues to consider when a child has AIDS:

• *Fear of Separation*

Fear of separation can be a real problem, since a child may already have experienced separation through hospitalization or the death of a parent.

- *Feeling Helpless*

Children are powerless in general and even more so in this situation. Asking the child's opinion and giving simple choices can help empower at least a little bit. "Do you want oatmeal or eggs and toast for breakfast?" may sound elemental, but it gives a choice, a small sense of victory.

- *Physical Changes*

A child with AIDS may suffer neurological damage that causes learning disabilities, lose weight, be generally fragile, both emotionally and physically, and, in general, look ill. This can be devastating to an adult and doubly so to a child. Again, reassure, reassure, reassure that the child is loved and precious and valuable. Reassure that she did not cause her illness. Reassure that her parents did not mean to infect her. Reassure that she will be listened to, her opinions valued, and her life considered important.

There are two good books for children whose family member dies of AIDS: *Losing Uncle Tim* by MaryKate Jordan and *Just a Heartbeat Away* by Gabriel Constans. Both explain the grief children experience. Both basically say that what is important is that love doesn't die and the person they loved was a good person. Local and state AIDS programs can also help with support groups and resources.

38

SUICICE

"They don't know what they do to us, they just don't know." A mother whose teenage son killed himself said it over and over at a suicide support group. And it's true. People who complete suicide often have expressed to others that their families and friends would be better off without them. They truly believe that by killing themselves they're doing us a favor. They don't realize the grief and guilt and stigma their death will bring.

Years ago, suicide became a religious issue. It was thought that one way to prevent suicide was to make it a sin. In the fourth century, church leaders thought people would be afraid of sinning and would not kill themselves. Nine hundred years later, church leaders tried to prevent suicide by making it a mortal sin for which the punishment was eternal damnation. In ancient times, if someone in your family completed suicide, you could actually have a brand placed on your body somewhere. In addition, you were shunned or not spoken to . . . you were scorned and ridiculed. None of these efforts worked, but this history has carried over into how some people still react, and it has contributed to people being afraid to talk about this form of death.

In fact, my hunch is that as you read this you stumbled a little over the new term "completed" suicide. We're used to saying "committed," as if it were a crime, and in some states it is actually on the books as just that—a crime. Of course the joke is how do you enforce it and what do you do to the people "committing" that crime? Kill them?

Things are better today than in ancient times. Today:

- Suicide is recognized as a physical/mental problem.
- There are suicide hotlines and prevention information.
- Almost all churches allow services and burial for suicide victims.
- More and more counselors, clergy, teachers, and doctors are studying suicide.

Vanessa, a twelve year old whose brother killed himself, was asked about it by friends just after she returned to school. The issue of religion came up and as usual the talk turned to myths of people being buried at crossroads and not in church cemeteries. Vampires even got into the picture and of course hell became a popular discussion item, too. Vanessa listened and smiled and then said, "The way our family looks at this is that Vinny gave his life back to God . . . period."

As with all forms of death, honesty is vital. As in the story of the grandmother earlier in this book, it's much better to hear the truth from family and friends than from classmates in a moment of meanness. To deny or to hide the suicide is to turn it into the skeleton in the closet, the elephant in the living room, and the family secret that is known by everyone.

What is important to your family is not the means of death, but the life that was lived. Make sure the children know they are not to blame in any way, that their loved one was very ill mentally and did not know things would get better some day. "She had a sickness in her head" was how one four year old explained her mother's death.

One of the most helpful ways of explaining suicide to a small child comes from Helen Fitzgerald in *The Grieving Child*. "Start by putting your child in a position where you are touching each other, perhaps on your lap. Children need lots of touching to feel secure. Tell her you have something very sad to tell her and that sometimes when one feels sad one cries, and that crying is okay. You might add that talking about this sad thing can make you cry and when you cry you need hugs. This will give her something to do when you cry and she will feel less frightened. Now you must go on to say, 'Daddy died today.'" Helen advises that you pause here. Usually a child will ask a question and you can go on. The question is usually going to be a "how?" question. Helen goes on, "Sometimes we can't understand why people die in the way they do." You can explain that when people have certain illnesses we can know how the illness caused their death, or if the person dies in an accident we can explain that, too. It's harder to explain that the person killed himself. Helen suggests, "Sometimes people do it to themselves. Do you know what that is called?" Here is a chance to use the word they will hear very soon, "suicide." You can say, "Sometimes people have an illness of the mind that makes them kill themselves. *They* have it, *you* don't, *I* don't. It's hard to understand and it has nothing to do with me or you. I didn't and you didn't do anything to cause this."

It's equally important to be honest about the means of death. "He took a gun and shot himself," or "She took a lot of pills all at once." Just as important as the honesty is the reassurance. "If Daddy loved me, why didn't he want to stay alive and be with me?" Justin asked. His mom replied, "Daddy loved you very, very much. His sickness in his mind didn't let him think right, though. He didn't know how much his dying would hurt all of us. I want you to know something else, too. Daddy knew how much you loved him, too."

Telling the child he will not meet the same fate can be important, too. Earl Grollman says, "Listen responsively. Your son may tell you he was cast in the same mold as the parent. He constantly recalls similarities, how they resembled each other both physically and mentally. Help the youngster understand the truth. There is no cruel seed of self-destruction lurking in him. The person who died is not the same person as the child who is beside you. Each individual is different. Suicidal tendencies are not bequeathed like family heirlooms.

"One of the things that really pushes my angry button is to hear a school official say his school doesn't allow memorial services for students who kill themselves because they don't want to glamorize it or encourage other students to be copycats. This denies the valid grief of surviving students, adds to the stigma of the death, and denigrates the life of the student who died, once again treating it like a crime instead of the result of mental illness. In addition, a tremendous teaching opportunity is lost forever. As if that isn't bad enough, almost every school that denies recognition of the student's death finds itself dealing with more fights on school property, more absenteeism, and more problems in general because students aren't allowed to express feelings in a safe way. We're finally beginning to pull the dark shroud of fear off suicide, just as we are with death in general. It's a good start."

39

~~~~~~

HOMICIDE

Traumatized. Victimized. Brutalized. Those are words that describe what happens to children who witness a homicide or whose family member is murdered. There are some events in our lives that are "measure-marks." Everything is spoken about and thought about as either before or after that event. Such it is with murder. When something so violent and brutal happens, we react. Children react, too.

In her compelling workbook for children, *Reactions to Trauma and Grief*, Alison Saloum says, "When someone close to you dies suddenly, or when you or someone else gets hurt, like shot or stabbed, you may experience different reactions. Reactions occur because of what has happened. There are emotional reactions, body reactions, and behavioral reactions. Emotional reactions are your feelings. Physical reactions are when your body responds to what has happened and behavioral reactions are how you act because of what has happened. These reactions may feel very scary, but they are normal when someone gets hurt or killed."

Wanda Henry-Jenkins, author of *Just Us: Homicidal Loss and Grief*, describes the complicated mourning that occurs in families and has a powerful impact on children. Wanda says the homicidal grief process has three cycles: crisis, conflict, and commencement. This is what happens:

Crisis	Conflict	Commencement
Death Notification	Mourning Delayed	Trial Ends
Autopsy		Holiday Blues
Identify Victim	Arrest	Closure on Business
Police Investigation	Preliminary Hearing	Mourning
Media Reports	Arraignments	Group Support
Funeral/Burial	Homicide Trial	Healing
Mourning Begins		Anniversaries
	or	
Shock (Numbness)	No Arrest	
Denial (Questioning)	Unsolved Murder	
Anger and Rage	Unfinished Business	Focus on the Living
Revenge	Acquittal	Pleasant Memories
Fear	Conviction	Happy Days
Anxiety	Sentencing	New Growth
Victim-Centered	Victim	Gradual Change
Sleep Problems	Impact Statement	Self-Oriented Thoughts
Appetite Problems		Longing
	Guilt	Relief
	Despair	
	Powerlessness	
	Abandonment	
	Bitterness	

It's easy to see that children involved in this unique grief can become terrified, enraged, and confused in addition to their normal grief reactions. There are three things to remember when it comes to guiding children through homicidal grief.

1. *Feeling Safe:* When the shots rang out, Cassie fell forward. She could feel her heart beating and she could hear other children screaming. She wasn't hurt, but she was a victim of one of the school shootings that took place in the United States in 1998. Her best friend died in the attack. Children who experience this kind of trauma are like victims of war. Luckily, most of our children don't experience enough of it to have the glassy-eyed stare we've seen in children from other lands where war wages around them daily. Cassie, however, learned early and learned the hard way that her world was no longer safe and secure.

   Our son Jim was married and had lived away from home for four years when he called us late one night. His best friend's father had been shot and killed by a burglar. "I just want you guys to be careful," Jim said. "Just be careful." I will never forget hearing the fear and concern in his voice. You don't have to be a little kid to have your world shattered and your fears aroused.

   Make sure there is someplace where the child can feel safe, whether that's at home in a certain room, at school, or at a church. If, tragically, there is no safe place, let the child draw an imaginary safe place and tell him he can go there at any time in his imagination.

2. *Being Touched:* Especially in smaller children, the need for touching and cuddling is very important.

This can be especially hard if you are a parent whose child or spouse has been murdered and you are dazed and feel as if you are encased in plastic. You, yourself, need more touching and cuddling right now. Make sure some time each day is spent holding the child on your lap, hugging, or just touching an almost-grown arm as you pass by. Remember: it is absolutely okay for you to ask for a hug from your child. Children of all ages need to feel there is something they can do to help.

3. *Looking Forward:* Remember the old book *Happiness Is a Warm Puppy?* One of the happiness statements was "Having Something to Look Forward To." Both children and adults need to see a future. We need to know that the shock and terror of what has happened will not always hound us. We need to know that life will move on. There will be happy memories and good days. There will be fun times and a future. We all need something to look forward to.

40

DRUNK DRIVERS

D runk driving fits immediately after homicide because it's not just "an accident." It's knowingly driving when you know it's not safe and you are endangering others. Each year thousands of people are killed and wounded by drunk drivers. Candy Lightner founded MADD (Mothers Against Drunk Driving) when her daughter was killed by a drunk driver who was a repeat offender. A part of the tragedy of drunk drivers is that families must frequently live with the fact that their loved one is dead and nothing very serious happened to the driver.

Everything that applies to children's needs in a homicidal death applies here, too. Teri is a good example. Her little brother was killed when an intoxicated driver sped through a stoplight and smashed into the side of the car where Danny was sitting, carefully seatbelted in. Teri's parents were devastated and so was she, but she made sure they attended the trial of the driver, wrote letters to the court, and appeared every day so the jury could see what "motor vehicle homicide" family victims looked like sitting in the courtroom.

Teri's story reflects the strength teens often display in a family crisis as well as the tension that can encircle a family. We've talked earlier about transcending grief. Frequently, children who experience a tragic death in their family work in groups such as Students Against Drunk Driving and on occasion dedicate their lives to such a cause both personally and professionally.

One of the elements of homicide in any form is the rage—not anger, rage—that seems to be a natural element of this type of grief. Helping children find a healthy outlet for that rage can be found in the service mentioned above, in active sports, writing, pounding on pillows, and talking, talking, talking about the experience and the effect it is having on them and their family.

41

~~~~~~

NATIONAL
TRAGEDIES

Our son-in-law Ben called me and said, "Turn on the TV. We've got news . . . big news." I turned the television on to see crowds of people running from the Murrah building in Oklahoma City. There had been reports of a second bomb.

Two years later when we went to Oklahoma City, the area around the bombing was like a war zone. As I was videotaping the area, Marv said, "You'd better talk so people will know where we are and what we're doing." I replied softly, "I can't talk." The lump in my throat was too huge.

As I was writing this section, I ran into Ben's office. As you know, Ben is our son-in-law who works with us. "What do you remember about being in school and watching the Challenger explode?" I asked. "Oh," Ben said, suddenly somber. "It was depressing; really, really depressing and sad. We'd brought a television into the room and we were cheering the lift off and then there was the explosion. There was total quiet, total shock. Then some people started crying. We were all paralyzed. We couldn't move."

I asked another question: "Do you remember it vividly, like it was yesterday?"

"It will always be like yesterday," Ben replied.

Even as a three year old, sitting in my high chair on a Sunday afternoon, I clearly remember how my parents stood and looked at each other, my mother beginning to cry, as the President of the United States announced that the Japanese had bombed Pearl Harbor. I was three!

I was nearly sixty when I climbed aboard the *Lisa Marie*, Elvis Presley's private jet. I remembered the early Elvis. I was a teenager. I had never been a tremendous fan, but I enjoyed his music, and when we did a workshop in Memphis, we toured Graceland. I was struck by the sense of loss and the many wreaths that arrived to grace the grave of the king. We grieve as a group.

I don't need to tell you that I remember what I wore, where I was, and exactly what I was doing when President John F. Kennedy was shot—or Bobby Kennedy—or Martin Luther King, Jr. When I walked through a department store the Sunday after J.F.K. died, there was no sound at all except for the television sets making us a part of a national tragedy. We were a nation in mourning. We have been so many times since.

And grief is now international. Princess Diana's funeral was watched by many more families than was Queen Elizabeth's coronation. No sooner had the announcer caught her breath describing the entourage to the cemetery for Diana than she read the bulletins reporting Mother Teresa's death.

This generation of children is the first to have instant news coverage through the now common television set. They are aware of their world in ways older generations could not contemplate. You can change the channel, but you can't change the event. Kids will talk to each other. They'll discuss events in class.

Including the children in this grief is just as important as including them in family grief, for we are a world family. Our world village is very small. We are all human. We all suffer together. One of the most touching columns I ever read in a newspaper was by a man who remembered being awakened in the early morning hours by his father, who simply got him dressed and took him to the depot in their small town. Many other townspeople had gathered on the platform, and as the little boy looked down the track he realized there were more people on both sides of the railroad. They stretched as far as he could see. Finally, from far away came the lonely whistle of the big train. All down the line men removed their hats and held them over their hearts. "What is it, Daddy?" the little boy asked. "Hold your head high, son," his father said, "the President is passing by." It was Franklin Delano Roosevelt's funeral train, draped in red, white, and blue, sounding its sorrowful wail to echo the grieving hearts of a nation in mourning.

Watching a televised Mass or memorial service as a family may be helpful at the time of tragedy. Talking about what happened and how these events are also a part of our lives can help, too. Sometimes just a quiet walk together with your children while you talk accomplishes a lot. "What do you think about all that?" is a good beginning question. As one ten-year-old boy said in response to that inquiry, "I think there are a lot of really bad people in the world who do really bad things. But I think there are a lot more really good people who do really super things. I'm glad we're some of the good ones."

CONCLUSION

I am very hopeful. Just a few years ago this book would not even have been considered by a publisher. Death was too frightening and the idea of teaching children about death and grief was taboo. Now more than 150 cities have full-time centers for grieving children and their families, there are hundreds of resources and support groups, and adults everywhere are coming to new terms in recognizing children as valuable young people who have much to teach us about emotions and grief and what is truly valuable in life.

Remember as you work with grieving children, whether your own or those of other parents, as you teach them and guide them through grief, you are changing their lives for the better. You are encouraging a great acceptance that life is not forever, that it is to be lived fully, and that sorrow and grief are a normal part of our existence. Whenever you comfort a child, you comfort yourself. Whenever you walk the journey of grief with a young person, you grow as well.

One of the questions in the Questions and Answers section of this book is one we are asked almost monthly: "Isn't it depressing to work with grieving children and adults?" Our answer is always "No." It's not depressing, it's enriching. It lets us see people in their realness, to share their sorrow and to realize once again that the only truly bereaved people are those who have never loved. May you love fully and richly and completely.

LET EXPERIENCE TEACH US: PROFESSIONALS IN THE FIELD

As I worked on this book, the big question began to lift its smiling face. "What does everybody else think is the most important key to teaching children about death and grief?" The simple solution: ask them. I had a delightful time on the telephone to several good, caring people and here's what they said:

Andrea Gambill publishes *Bereavement Magazine*. Her daughter Judy died in an automobile accident.

As adults we are conditioned to tell children what they should do, feel, think, and believe. If we can free ourselves from this conditioning, we find it virtually revolutionary to listen to what children have to tell us. They know what they feel, but often don't know the names of their feelings. They can't tell us they feel anxious or guilty or impatient. They can tell us they are sad or afraid, but if we're not truly listening, they can't tell us why in terms we can understand.

Children have so much to teach us about their lives and needs and we need to be willing to listen, not only with our ears but with our minds and hearts as well. We need to get on their level both physically and emotionally. We need to pay attention to their body and play language. When we take off our masks of authority and power and get down and play with them on the floor, they can often communicate more clearly as Ken or Barbie or Superman than they can as Suzy or Johnny. We can hear them if we're listening with our hearts and with our own inner child. Their message is honest and lovely and pure. When we are truly listening, we can truly learn. Only then can we truly help.

Rabbi Earl Grollman, whose outstanding book *Talking About Death: A Dialogue Between Parent and Child* is one of the great classics in bereavement literature, is a leading lecturer and writer on death and grief. Earl says:

The most important thing is to develop the ability to ask questions that are open ended so children can share. This means not to say, "How are you?" or "What's happening?" but questions that require longer answers, such as "You don't seem to be yourself. What's going through your mind?" "When you think of her, what comes to your mind?" and "What do you wish you had done?" Let them know you're not there to tell them anything, you're there to listen. I tell kids that they're my teacher and they love that. They really respond.

Linda Goldman wrote *Life and Loss: Breaking the Silence* and *Bart Speaks Out—An Interactive Story Book for Young Children on Suicide.* Linda tells us:

The most important key in teaching children about death and grief is not to teach them anything but to allow them to express what they are feeling about it and give them an open environment to express what they feel. They are so good at teaching us, so allow them to teach us where they are with their grief. Every child is unique and so is their grief. How we can teach them is to serve as models ourselves, and if we can grieve openly and allow kids that experience and expression, that's the greatest teaching.

Dan Schaefer is a lecturer, hypnotist, and superb writer. His book *How Do We Tell the Children?* is one of the outstanding resources for parents and caregivers. Dan's answer is:

Turn your back and look at the kid's environment. You can spend five hours a day with a child nurturing and loving him, but if the environment isn't appropriate, the kid is going to be under continuous pressure. Turning your back isn't meant to be harsh, it just means that there is more than just the child involved. The child needs anchors, which means that everywhere the child goes, there needs to be someone there who knows about a grieving child. You can't heal the grieving child. You can only create a nurturing environment. Once you figure out you can't take a child's grief away, you can begin to help him. A kid is like a flower. You've got to water and then let 'em grow. Kids need permission to grieve, examples of grief, freedom to grieve.

Helen Fitzgerald is director of the first grief program in the nation that was established in a community health center. She has worked with hundreds of children and wrote the wonderful book *The Grieving Child.*

What's so important about starting with children at an early age is that they grow up learning the words and ways to grieve. I get calls from people who have teens and all at once are telling them about a death that occurred a long time ago. Inform children at a young age, using age-appropriate language. We have a four-year-old child in our group who knows his father died by his own hand. He said, "Did Daddy want to die?" Mom said, "Yes, he did." Now he's beginning to ask the questions. He won't have any sur-

prises. There are still a lot of people who think children should be protected and that's not so.

Jacque Bell has been a child-life coordinator in a medical setting for 20 years, working with hundreds of families whose children are hospitalized and with children whose loved one has died. Jacque tells us:

Don't be afraid of the questions that might come or of the answers you might give. Talking from your gut is probably the best thing you can do. Spontaneous responses are really okay. Seek out an expert if you need one, but remember that inclusion of the child in the entire process is more important than worry and exclusion. Often the child's fantasy is worse than the reality and not including her as part of the bereavement process is just a recipe for short- and long-term problems. Excluding and worrying about whether what you're doing is right or wrong may miss those teachable moments. And when those teachable moments do come, give information out in small doses as the questions arise. Don't overwhelm a child all at once with more than she needs or wants to know.

Beverly Chappell is one of the pioneers working with and loving grieving children. She founded The Dougy Center in Portland, Oregon, the first full-time center for grieving children.

Be open and honest with them. Let them be a part of anything they see in their environment that is dead—even possums in the road or birds on the sidewalk. Don't keep things from them. Don't pretend nothing is happening if someone in the family is dying. After a death, let them participate in anything in which they feel comfortable, at the same time explaining thoroughly what they will see and what it will be like when they view the body, or attend the wake or funeral itself. Don't put pictures of their loved per-

son away and pretend the person never existed. Keep memories alive. That is the part of the person they carry in their hearts.

Gail Cinelli is the executive director of the Center for Grieving Children in Portland, Maine. Gail was a contributor to the book *Thank You for Coming to Say Goodbye*.

Children need to know the truth. They can handle the truth no matter how hard, and they're ready and waiting to share their feelings when you give them a safe place. They teach all of us and everyone around us. Children are our teachers. This is what we've learned here. This is what we learn every day—from children and teens.

Nancy Crump is a grief counselor for D.W. Newcomer's Sons Funeral Homes in Kansas City, Missouri. She conducts a suicide survivor's group and is especially good with children.

First, I would identify things we grieve over—anyone or anything we value and no longer have. Second, I would normalize grief reactions—just don't hurt yourself or others—and let them know some of the types of reactions they might experience. Third, I would let them know that even though grief lasts a lifetime—as long as we have memory— given time and the opportunity to work on our grief, it gets easier to cope. Fourth, I would give them some practical tips on how to work on their grief—talking about their loss, allowing themselves to feel what they feel—and some activities to help themselves along the way. I would also make them aware that there may be special times as they are growing up that their grief may reappear—such as when they learn to drive a car, go to their first dance or on their first date, graduate from high school, get married, have children, and other times, too.

After the Oklahoma City bombing, Danny Mize responded to the children. Danny is the executive director and cofounder of The Kids' Place, a children's grief-support center.

Children need to know that death is a natural and normal part of the "package" of life. We can begin when they are very young, pointing out to them the concept of life and death in their world. We can explain the cycle of life and death in nature—plants and pets are good beginning points. As they grow and mature, we can explain that people die (their bodies stop working).

Louise Vance is Centering Corporation's bereavement consultant. She is part of the staff at the New Song Center in Phoenix. Louise points out:

It can really be pretty simple when it comes to supporting and guiding children through grief. Listen to them. Be honest with them. Share your feelings. Allow their feelings. Answer their questions. Love them.

Reverend Richard Gilbert is the executive director of The World Pastoral Care Center. He has written extensively and reviewed the majority of resources on grief as well as presented workshops across the United States and Canada.

What is most important for parents and caregivers is twofold. One, that children are grieving, struggling with feelings, questions, worries about family and self, and a longing for something spiritual that brings meaning, hope, and safety. Second, and this is equally important, children do not need you to "take care of them." Rather, they want you to walk with them, grieve with them, play with them, talk with them. If you journey together, you may just be surprised and pleased with the comfort, insight, and hope children can bring to you.

Carol Dannen has been Centering Corporation's consultant for nearly 25 years. Carol tells us:

Grief and loss cut across all religions and beliefs. I think the most important thing to tell families is to trust your feelings and be willing to let them go when new feelings come. Whether pet or person, every living thing you know has touched you in some way. What you carry forward of that person is like a legacy or gift they have given you and it's a way they have of going on living. So take time to collect those items and memories of your lost loved one because that is what you'll keep forever.

The real experts aren't all of us who have written and lectured and conducted workshops around the world. The real experts on teaching children about death and grief are the children themselves. They are the ones who take our hands and lead us down the road of knowledge. Children are the ones who show us how to express our emotions honestly, to ask the tough questions, to look at people closely to discern whether what they are telling us is true and honest or a feeble attempt to protect when it's not needed. The real experts are those parents who are willing to show emotions, model grief by sharing their tears and other feelings, and fumble through the tough questions by answering from their gut or by being brave enough to say, "I don't know." The real experts are those of you who listen to the children and let them tell you their fears and feelings and ideas. As Jeanne Harper, author of *Hurting Yourself*, says, "When a child asks, 'What happens after you die?' only an idiot, only a grown-up would answer. The real answer is 'I'm not sure just what happens. What do you think?' And you're in for a lecture." Go for it!

QUESTIONS AND ANSWERS

What if my child doesn't want to talk about death?

Be gentle and honor your child's feelings. Mention things quietly, speak of death as normal. If you are teaching through everyday death experiences, such as finding a dead bird on the sidewalk, then simply do what you think appropriate and allow the child to watch. Wrap the bird in leaves, talking out loud as you do so. Gently bury the bird. Sing a song if you want. The child doesn't have to participate to learn a lot.

What if I'm trying to teach after a family member has died and the child resists?

That's different. If he covers his ears and runs into another room, you have a more difficult task. Follow him, don't leave him alone. Be reassuring and say something like, "I know this is hard to talk and think about, but it's really not all that scary. I know you have a lot of questions, and when you're ready to talk I'll be here." Cuddling helps at this point, too.

Should my child attend the funeral?

We think that families who love together grieve together. Grief is a family affair, and children should be allowed to be involved in and part of funerals from the earliest possible age.

159

What if my child doesn't want to go to the funeral?

Explain, as we have above, that this is something your family needs to do together, that you or someone else close to the child will be with her at all times. If, however, she is adamant about not wanting to go, don't force her. Be sure she has a loving and safe place to stay where she won't get guilt messages for not wanting to attend.

Every time I try to explain why Grammy died, I start to cry and my seven-year-old son gets upset. What should I do?

Hold your little boy on your lap and tell him you're going to cry and that's okay. He's not making you cry and crying helps you get the sad out. Tell him that if he wants to cry with you that's okay, too. It's important that he know grief and tears in grown-ups is all right and that you're willing to struggle through a lot of tears to tell him what he needs to know.

My nine year old has nightmares since her older brother died and wants to get into bed with us every night. Should we let her?

Certainly. This is a frightening time. Let her know that bad dreams are a part of grieving. Ask her to tell you about the dreams as well. The next day ask her to draw her dream for you. One little girl drew her dead mother but had only a huge head in the picture. When her father asked how she could make the dream better, she said simply, "Give Mommy her body back." She drew the rest of her mother's body and the dreams stopped.

Why should I ruin my child's innocence and enjoyment of life by teaching him about death and grief?

Because death and grief are a part of life and your child won't be innocent for long. Today's television news will show international disasters, shootings, and other means of death. By the time a child reaches third grade, he has seen hundreds of deaths on television.

How can I explain the difference between television show death, such as Road Runner and Wile E. Coyote and even some of the more adult shows, and real life?

You can use the language of pretend. Tell your child these people only pretend to be dead, that in real life there is great sadness when a loved one dies, that when someone kills another person, they are punished very severely. And as always, let the child ask questions. There are many teachable moments on television. We can use them well.

My daughter seems obsessed by death. She asks about it everyday and even buried one of her dolls. Is this normal?

It's not unusual. At some point almost every child becomes aware of death and is very curious and imaginative. It's a way of coming to terms with this aspect of life.

Isn't it depressing working with and being around people who are grieving?

Not at all. It's enriching. The stories people have to tell are real and touching and when people are grieving they are at their most genuine.

My teenager's best friend died and now he's driving fast and I suspect he's drinking. What can I do?

Share your concerns and share them strongly. That doesn't mean to yell at him and accuse him. Rather, tell him you're afraid. Ask him how he can help you, and if you're still worried, talk to his school counselor.

161

My children are teens or older and don't want their brother mentioned during the holidays. He's been dead for several years, but I don't want to forget him and I want to honor him.

Hang the stockings as usual. Put a special ornament on the tree. Mention his name in a fun memory once or twice while the family is together. Privately, it may be your time to go through pictures, burn a candle, cry again, and write him a letter. One mother wrote her son a letter a day from December first to Christmas day. She put all the letters in his stocking; then, after all the family had gone home, she burned them in her fireplace, watching the smoke go toward heaven and taking messages of her love with it.

My little boy keeps thinking his daddy will come home. He's only four years old. How can I convince him Daddy's not coming back?

You can't. Children this age don't have a concept of permanence. They can't get a handle on "never" yet. As he grows older, he'll have more questions and will slowly come to realize that he will never see his daddy again. That doesn't mean he'll forget him. It's important to keep those memories alive, even though Daddy isn't.

What is the most important key you think parents and caregivers need in teaching children about death and grief?

It's important to have an open mind and an open heart, and the desire to listen to them and not try to fix it because you can't "fix" it. It's important to be a companion to the child through the grief and to share your own grief. It doesn't hurt, either, if you have a good sense of humor and you love to laugh.

GLOSSARY

Acceptance the feeling that comes when at last we realize the death is real, the person is not coming back, and our lives will go on

Acting out usually unacceptable behavior that develops from unexpressed or stuffed feelings

Advocacy standing up for and directing others in ways to help your grieving child and family

AIDS acquired immune deficiency syndrome—a disease that is eventually fatal, although new treatments are very promising

Anger the feeling of mini-rage that accompanies grief

Bereavement literally means: to be torn apart, to have special needs, to be cheated. It is the entire syndrome of grief and mourning.

Bereavement counselors therapists specially trained to work with grieving persons

Bereavement patterns the ways in which we grieve and mourn, often taught by family custom

Blocking refusing to allow grief in

Body donation a body is given to a medical school for study, then returned to the family as **cremains**

Burial placing the body in the ground, usually in a casket, which is then placed inside a vault

Casket the box that holds the body

Cemetery a burial place

Child life specialist a professional, usually working in a hospital setting, who supports children during their own or other family member's hospitalization

Child's visitation a special time when children can come to the funeral home, view the body, and ask questions of the funeral director

Chronic illness a lingering or recurring sickness that does not necessarily end in death

Clingy the behavior that comes from the need to be constantly near and touching someone to promote a sense of safety and reduce anxiety

Closed casket a service in which the body is present in the casket but the casket is closed and the body not seen

Commemorate to perform a ceremony or ritual that remembers the dead person

Complicated mourning grief that is extended and intensified by various factors and takes longer to resolve

Concepts ideas or beliefs

Coping skills ways and means with which to deal with crisis and trauma

Cremains the ash that is left after cremation

Cremation a means of disposing of the body through intense heat, which turns the body into a fine ash

Cultural norm the way of mourning that is adapted and followed by a family for more than one generation

Deactivating turning off in order to replace with something new

Death education teaching what happens to the body after a person dies

Denial the inability to admit that the death happened. As with other feelings, this one comes and goes.

Depression continuing sadness and feeling "down" or "blue"

Embalming exchanging a special preservative liquid with the dead person's blood

Emotion commotion room a special room, usually found in centers for grieving children, where children can hit a punching bag, throw things at the wall, and release anger and other emotions safely

Emotions the feelings that come when we experience grief and mourning

Empathy being able to feel *with* someone as opposed to feeling *for* someone

Funeral the special service at which we remember and say goodbye to the person who died, usually held one to seven days after the death

Funeral director a trained professional who helps the family plan and conduct the final services for the person who has died

Funeral home the place where bodies are taken and cared for before the funeral or memorial service

Funeral procession the long, sad parade of cars that go from the funeral home to the cemetery

Grave the hole dug in the warm earth that holds the body, casket, and vault

Grief the thoughts and feelings we have when someone we love dies

Grief companion one who walks with a child or adult on the journey of grief, who is a good listener, and who provides support and comfort

Grief education teaching about the emotions that may come after a loss

Guilt the feeling that we are responsible for something bad

Headstone that which marks the grave of the person and tells the person's name, date of birth, and date of death

HIV human immunodeficiency virus—the virus that causes AIDS

Homicide murder—the intentional killing of another person

Hospice an organization that provides home care and instructions for families whose loved ones want to die at home

Inclusion   involving the children in the planning and completion of the funeral or memorial service

Journaling   writing down your feelings on a regular basis, creating your own grief book

Magical thinking   thoughts children have when they believe that if they think it, it will happen

Memorial service   a gathering of family and friends to remember the person who died, share stories, and comfort one another, which can be held at any time after the death

Mental illness   diagnosed emotional problems, of which grief is not one

Mommy/Daddy Box   a special box that holds mementos of parents who have died

Mourning   the outward expression of grief

Open casket   a funeral or memorial service where the casket is open and the body can be seen or viewed

Organ donation   the giving of usable parts of the body such as the heart, lungs, and eyes to be removed just after death and transplanted to a living person

Pathological illness   illness that is genetic or physical in nature

Red flags   a term used to identify complicated mourning and danger signals in grieving children; indicates the need for professional help

Regression   retreating into youthful, childlike behavior to bring comfort and security

Ritual   a specific series of actions or behaviors performed for a particular reason

School counselors   professionals who are part of the school system who work with children in many areas, including grief and trauma

Shock   the feeling of numbness and disbelief that comes when first hearing about the death of a loved one and that may occur at later times as well

Sorrow   the feeling of sadness that comes with loss, often accompanied by crying

Suicide   taking one's own life—killing yourself

Superstitions   beliefs resulting from fear of the unknown, a mistaken idea of why things happen, or a trust in magic or the supernatural

Terminal illness   a sickness that ends in death

Theologian   one who studies religious beliefs

Theology   the body of religious beliefs held by individuals and churches

Transactional analysis   a form of self-help psychology that recognizes the parent, adult, and child in each of us

Trauma   an emergency that results in panic, anxiety, and intense emotional reactions; can also be a physical injury

Urn   the container that holds the cremains

Vault   the strong, concrete box that holds the casket in the ground

Victim's impact statement   written information for the court of how the homicide affected the family of the victim

Viewing   a time when family and friends gather, usually a day or so before the funeral, when the body can be seen in the casket

Wailers   people in ancient times who were hired to weep and make loud, sad noises at funerals

Wake   a watch over the body of the dead person; often includes sharing good memories and enjoying family times

167

RECOMMENDED READING AND RESOURCES

Today there are many books, videos, and other tools available for grieving children and their families. We've listed just a few. Several are classics, others are brand new.

General
Preschool to Age Six

Blackburn, Lynn. *I Know I Made It Happen*. Omaha, NE: Centering Corporation, 1991. (Here's the one that takes care of the worries of magical thinking and deals with the unrealistic guilt children often experience.)

Brown, Margaret Wise. *The Dead Bird*. New York: Harper, 1938. (One of the first books about death written for children. It's a wonderful classic and has gone in and out of print several times. Now it's here to stay.)

Ferguson, Dorothy. *A Bunch of Balloons*. Omaha, NE: Centering Corporation, 1992. (A workbook for very young children. Compares death to letting go of a balloon. Shows the child she has many people left.)

Greenlee, Sharon. *When Someone Dies*. Atlanta, GA: Peachtree Publishers, 1992. (Probably the single most beautiful book on both death and grief and for all ages.)

Johnson, Joy, and Marv Johnson. *Tell Me, Papa*. Omaha, NE: Centering Corporation, 1978. (The first child's book explaining death and funerals. Another classic.)

Mellonie, Bryan, and Robert Ingpen. *Lifetimes*. New York: Bantam Books, 1983. (This is the basic teaching book about death for young children. Beautiful pictures, simple text. More about death than about grief.)

Six to Twelve

Brown, Laurie, and Marv Brown. New York: Little Brown, 1996. *When Dinosaurs Die*. (This is a delightful book of cartoons that covers every feeling and question a child could have.)

O'Toole, Donna. *Aarvy Ardvark Finds Hope*. Burnsville, NC: Compassion Books, 1989. (Colorful and easy reading. General, even though it involves the loss of a mother.)

Rofes, Eric, and The Fayerweather Street School Staff. *The Kids' Book About Death and Dying*. New York: Little Brown, 1985. (Read it in the kids' own words. To the point and very well done.)

Traisman, Enid. *A Child Remembers*. Omaha, NE: Centering Corporation, 1994. (A gentle workbook for a grieving child.)

Especially for Teens

Bode, Janet. *Death Is Hard to Live With*. New York: Bantam, 1993. (Exceptional book where all kinds of deaths are discussed. One of the best.)

Grollman, Earl. *Straight Talk About Death for Teenagers*. Boston, MA: Beacon Press, 1993. (Earl Grollman might well be called "Grandfather Grief" and here is his grandfather wisdom in language all teens can understand and love.)

Gunther, John. *Death Be Not Proud.* New York: Harper Collins, 1949, 1998. (One of the earliest books on grief. Good and very inspirational.)

Scrivani, Mark. *When Death Walks In.* Omaha, NE: Centering Corporation, 1991. (The basic book explaining death to adolescents. Great teen artwork.)

Sieff, Janet, and Enid Traisman. *Flowers for the Ones You've Known; Letters from Teens.* Omaha, NE: Centering Corporation, 1995. (Very vivid and touching, with various adolescents' art as well.)

Traisman, Enid. *Fire in My Heart; Ice in My Veins.* Omaha, NE: Centering Corporation, 1992. (A very popular guided journal for adolescents.)

Death of a Parent
Young Children

Clifton, Lucille. *Everett Anderson's Goodbye.* New York: Henry Holt, 1983. (Winner of the Coretta Scott King award, this is one of the most beautiful books available on death of a father.)

Scrivani, Mark.
I Heard Your Mommy Died
I Heard Your Daddy Died. Omaha, NE: Centering Corporation, 1992. (Two books, each of which gives excellent ideas such as saving the parent's T-shirts to wear as sleep shirts, gathering a box of special things to remember.)

Ages Six and Up

Hemery, Kathleen Maresh. *The Brightest Star.* Omaha, NE: Centering Corporation, 1998. (Winner: Parent Council Award. Death of a mother with active father figure and supportive teacher.)

Lowden, Stephanie Golightly. *Emily's Sadhappy Season.* Omaha, NE: Centering Corporation, 1993. (Takes a look at a present-day, confident little girl whose father dies suddenly.)

Tiffault, Benette. *A Quilt for Elizabeth.* Omaha, NE: Centering Corporation, 1992. (After Elizabeth's father dies her grandmother teaches her quilting, using Daddy's old clothes. Won a five-tissue award in a storytelling event.)

Death of a Sibling
Young Children

Goldstein, Heather, Ray Goldstein, and Jody Goldstein. *Where's Jess?* Omaha, NE: Centering Corporation, 1982. (The classic book for preschoolers when a baby sister or brother dies.)

Sims, Alicia. *Am I Still a Sister?* Louisville, KY: Big A And Co., 1986. (One of the first books actually written by a young, surviving sibling. It's still the best.)

Temes, Roberta. *The Empty Place.* Far Hills, NJ: Small Horizons, 1997. (There's an empty place at the table and in a little brother's heart. Very good.)

Vann Wesson. *Painting Sunsets with the Angels.* San Diego, CA: Orion Media, 1996. (After David dies, his family notices the beautiful sunsets with David's name painted in them. Spiritual in nature and quite nice.)

Death of a Grandparent

Often the first death a child experiences, these are good teaching tools.

Grandmothers

Coleman, Paul. *Where the Balloons Go.* Omaha, NE: Centering Corporation, 1996. (Corey's grandma loved balloons and said all loose balloons go to a beautiful balloon forest. After she dies, Corey tries to go to the balloon forest.)

de Paola, Tommie. *Nana Upstairs and Nana Downstairs.* New York: Penguin, 1973. (Here's the original book on death of a grandmother and still the only book that includes a great-grandmother. A true classic and very beautiful.)

Evarts, Dawn Michelle. *The Butterfly Bush.* Omaha, NE: Centering Corporation, 1998. (It was just a bundle of sticks, but it turned into a beautiful butterfly bush and created tender memories for a grandchild. Parents Council Award winner.)

Marshall, Bridget. *Animal Crackers.* Omaha, NE: Centering Corporation, 1998. (A little girl remembers her nanny and the animal crackers she used to hide. At Nanny's funeral, everyone gets a box of animal crackers to share along with happy memories. Parent Council Award winner.)

Grandfathers

Dickerson, Julie. *Grandpa's Berries.* Johnstown, PA: Cherubic Press, 1995. (The taste of the berry is as sweet as the memories of Grandpa. Excellent for little girls.)

Hodge, John. *Finding Grandpa Everywhere.* Omaha, NE: Centering Corporation, 1999. (It's hard to understand when Mom says "Grandma lost Grandpa," because Grandpa was so big—how could he get lost? But after the little boy in the story realizes Grandpa is dead, not lost, he finds him everywhere, including in his own heart.)

Morning, Barbara. *Grandfather's Shirt.* Omaha, NE: Centering Corporation, 1994. (When Grandpa dies, his gardening partner, Peter, gets the old shirt Grandpa wore. A lot of memories go with that shirt as Peter grows up.)

Death of a Pet

Johnson, Joy. *Remember Rafferty*. Omaha, NE: Centering Corporation, 1991. (Rafferty is a huge old dog who dies. Talks about feelings, has a memory journal for kids.)

Rylant, Cynthia. *Dog Heaven*. New York: Blue Sky Press, 1995. (Dogs can stay as long as they like in heaven and can be there when old friends—like us—show up. Cynthia also wrote *Cat Heaven*, which is the same as *Dog Heaven* only there's a lot of meowing going on.)

For Parents, Teachers, Clergy, and other Caregivers

Fitzgerald, Helen. *The Grieving Child*. New York: Fireside Books, 1992. (A great book written by another pioneer in the field of grief. A classic.)

Huntley, Theresa. *Helping Children Grieve*. Minneapolis, MN: Augsburg, 1991. (A truly great book. Excellent for teachers.)

Kushner, Harold. *When Bad Things Happen to Good People*. New York: Avon, 1981. (Answers the perennial question expressed in the title. This book has helped a lot of people through their spiritual questions.)

Johnson, Joy, and Marvin Johnson. *Children Grieve, Too*. Omaha, NE: Centering Corporation, 1998. (A very small, concise book that lists what to do and concepts according to age.)

Schaefer, Dan, and Christine Lyons. *How Do We Tell the Children?* New York: Newmarket Press, 1993. (One of the best books available. Even has a crisis section on words to use at the time of death.)

Violent Death

Henry-Jenkins, Wanda. *Just Us and the Hard Work Journal*. Omaha, NE: Centering Corporation, 1991, 1999. (For adults who experience grief from homicide.)

Loftis, Chris. *The Boy Who Sat by the Window*. Far Hills, NJ: Small Horizons, 1997. (A truly valuable and touching book, especially for children who experience after-school shootings or violence near schools.)

Salloum, Alison. *Reactions to Trauma and Grief*. Omaha, NE: Centering Corporation, 1999. (A fabulous workbook for children who have witnessed violence or whose family member is a victim of violence.)

Especially for Schools

Braden, Majel. *Grief Comes to Class*. Omaha, NE: Centering Corporation, 1992. (Very practical and clear with a case study included.)

Goldman, Linda. *Life and Loss*. Bristol, PA: Accelerated Development, 1994. (One of the really great books with one of the best and clearest formats anywhere.)

Hospice of Lancaster County. *A Teacher's Guide to the Grieving Student*. Lancaster, PA: Hospice, 1995. (Truly helpful and filled with good suggestions.)

Miller, Karen. *The Crisis Manual*. Beltsville, MD: Gryphon House, 1996. (A huge and fantastic tool for teachers and counselors. Covers everything from death grief to abuse. You'll fill this with tiny yellow Post-Its and notes to mark the many places you need.)

O'Toole, Donna. *Growing Through Grief*. Burnsville, NC: Compassion Books, 1989. (A wonderful, thorough, and totally safe K–12 curriculum. Many activities and teaching tools.)

Roberts, Janice. *Thank You for Coming to Say Goodbye*. Omaha, NE: Centering Corporation, 1996. (A step-by-step guide to funerals, funeral homes, and grief by the originator of children's funeral home visitations.)

Videos and Other Tools

Children Grieve, Too. Omaha, NE: Centering Corporation, 1998. (Experts from all across the United States discuss what grieving children need and what adults need to know about grieving children.)

My Friends Dolls. Omaha, NE: Centering Corporation. (These three-feet-tall dolls have four Velcro faces reflecting children's feelings: anger, sorrow, fear, and happiness. Used in schools, hospitals, hospices, and lots of other places, too.)

Rainbow's Remedy. Eloise Cole, Phoenix, AZ: Creative Resources for Death Education, 1992. (Rainbow the Clown shows us exactly what grief is like. Then her other self, Eloise, interviews families who have experienced various kinds of death.)

Standing Tall. Omaha, NE: Centering Corporation, 1995. (Seven teens tell what it is like when someone they love dies.)

INDEX

PARENTING KEYS JUST FOR PARENTS AND PARENTS-TO-BE!

Keys to...

Adopting a Child

Becoming a Father

Breast Feeding

Calming the Fussy Baby

Child Safety and Care of Minor Injuries

Childhood Illnesses

Children's Nutrition

Children's Sleep Problems

Choosing Childcare

Dealing with Bullies

Dealing with Childhood Allergies

Dealing with Stuttering

Disciplining Your Young Child

Helping Children Deal With Death and Grief

Interfaith Parenting

Investing in Your Child's Future

Parenting a Child with a Learning Disability

Parenting a Child with Attention Deficit Disorder

Parenting a Child with Down Syndrome

Parenting an Adopted Child

Parenting the Asthmatic Child

Parenting the Child with Autism

Parenting the Child with Cerebral Palsy

Parenting the Gifted Child

Parenting the Only Child

Parenting Twins

Parenting Your Anxious Child

Parenting Your Four-Year-Old

Parenting Your Five-Year-Old

Parenting Your One-Year-Old

Parenting Your Teenager

Parenting Your Three-Year-Old

Parenting Your Two-Year-Old

Preparing and Caring for Your Newborn

Preparing and Caring for Your Second Child

Raising a Deaf Child

Raising a Drug Free Child

Single Parenting

Successful Music Lessons

Successful Stepfathering

Successful Stepmothering

Teaching Children About God

Toilet Training

Your Child's Healthy Sexuality

Each Key: Paperback, $5.95 & $6.95 (Canada $7.95 & $9.50)

Books may be purchased at your bookstore, or by mail from Barron's. Enclose check or money order for total amount plus sales tax where applicable and 15% for postage and handling (minimum charge $4.95). Prices are subject to change without notice.

Barron's Educational Series, Inc.
250 Wireless Boulevard
Hauppauge, NY 11788
Call toll free: 1-800-645-3476
Visit our website at:
www.barronseduc.com

BARRON'S

(#39) R 3/99

In Canada:
Georgetown Book Warehouse
34 Armstrong Avenue
Georgetown, Ontario L7G 4R9
Call toll free: 1-800-247-7160